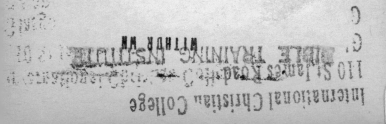

TEN INNER-CITY CHURCHES

WITHDRAWN

BIBLE TRAINING INSTITUTE

110 St James Road

International Christian College

TEN
INNER-CITY
CHURCHES

Edited by
Michael Eastman

MARC
British Church Growth Association
Evangelical Coalition for Urban Mission

The BCGA gratefully acknowledges the help of the Drummond Trust.

Unless otherwise noted, Bible quotations in this publication are from the Good News Bible © American Bible Society, 1976.

British Library Cataloguing in Publication Data

Ten inner-city churches.
  1. City clergy—Great Britain
  I. Eastman, Michael
  262'.14'0941   BV637.5

  ISBN 0–86065–627–6 (MARC)
      0–948704–11–X (BCGA)
      0–946842–03–5 (ECUM)

  Typeset for MARC, an imprint of Kingsway Publications, Lottbridge Drove, Eastbourne, E. Sussex BN23 6NT by Watermark, Hampermill Cottage, Watford WD1 4PL. Printed by Richard Clay Ltd, Bungay, Suffolk.

CONTENTS

ACKNOWLEDGEMENTS

There's a story behind every book. The ten contributors didn't know half of what lay before them when they agreed to put their stories in writing! My thanks to them for making time, often under unforeseen pressures, to share their experiences.

Without Lizzie Gibson of Kingsway, this book would never have reached the printers. Her sensitive editing and sympathetic but firm encouragement has sustained all of us. We owe her our gratitude for bringing it all together.

God is at work in our inner cities and outer estates. We who have experienced this first hand know that he is the source and sustainer of all that we tell.

We offer this to his praise and the encouragement of his church.

Michael Eastman

FOREWORD

Gandhi reflected upon his greatest problem and publicly confessed that it had been 'the hard-heartedness of the educated'. I identify with that. My inner-city experiences touch me deeply, but even more so when I am misunderstood. My own experience of hurt and pain is echoed in these pages, but also the excitement of real incarnational communication—the true living out of the Gospel. The ten churches here have made many slips and falls, fumbles and tumbles—but have also seen many flashes of spiritual success.

Exploring shalom, reaching working-class men, praying the Kingdom, setting up Good News structures, meeting faith and the faithless in the city, 'having a go' at the vicar identifying with the poor—all are here between layers of tension and emotional numbness.

Read and hear what the Spirit is saying and doing in the churches. Let us be quick to listen and slow to disagree as we soften our hearts, as we 'seek the shalom of the city, because in its shalom you shall find your own shalom' (Jeremiah 29:7).

Pip Wilson

**TEN
INNER-CITY
CHURCHES**

1 The Church at the Centre, Skelmersdale, Lancs
2 East Belfast Methodist Mission, Newtownards Road, Belfast
3 Bonneville Baptist Church, Lambeth, London
4 The Parish of Bestwood, Nottingham
5 St Peter's Church, Cardiff
6 Limehouse Parish Church, St Anne's, London
7 Aston Parish Church, Ss Peter & Paul, Birmingham
8 St John's, Park, Sheffield
9 Plaistow Christian Fellowship, Newham, London
10 St Agnes, Burmantofts, Leeds

Introduction

Michael Eastman

Michael Eastman is no casual observer, coolly looking down from some remote glass tower over the squalor and sadness that characterise so many inner cities today. On the contrary, as one who for the last twenty years has regularly visited and stayed in every major British conurbation, Michael knows first-hand the issues facing God's people. He packs his introduction with details about the current urban scene, but he does not leave us with mere depressing facts; instead he points us through his agenda to what urban priority area churches could be like. He infects us with enthusiasm for the ten stories that follow—stories of hope amid hopelessness.

Michael acted as one of the advisors to the Archbishop's Commission on Urban Priority Areas to whose report Faith in the City *he and many of the contributors refer. He serves as secretary to both the Evangelical Coalition for Urban Mission and Frontier Youth Trust (one of the Scripture Union's associated ministries), and is married with two grown daughters. He enjoys cricket and hill-walking.*

Tough task

Faith in the City exploded in a blaze of public controversy
on the British national scene the first weekend of December 1985. Attempts by a high government source
(never named) to rubbish it before publication
boomeranged. This report of the Archbishop's Commission on Urban Priority Areas touched a raw nerve in our
political life but gained widespread public sympathy. Following its acceptance by the Church of England General
Synod, the Catholic bishops and the Free Church Federal
Council adopted its findings. Britain's inner cities continue
to nag away at the national and church conscience; they
were one of the major issues at the 1987 general election.
The commission used the term urban priority areas (UPAs)
'to include inner-city districts and many large corporation
estates and other areas of high social deprivation'.[1]

The task of mission and ministry in such areas is the
toughest challenge facing the churches in Britain. It has
been so for 200 years, since the Industrial Revolution gave
birth—first in Britain—to the industrial city. 'In the century
of industrial development from 1831 to 1931 the percentage
of the British population living in areas classified as urban
rose from 34 to 80 and now stands at 90 per cent.'[2] The task
of mission and ministry in such areas is also an international
challenge. Ours is a rapidly increasing urban world. 'By the
year 2000 the number of large, multi-million cities will have
doubled from 29 to 58.'[3] If past trends continue, by then

> Mexico City might have 31 million inhabitants, São Paulo 26
> million, and New York 24 million ... Human multiplication is
> mostly beyond Europe in the poorer continents of Asia, Latin
> America and Africa, and within these areas the cities are grow-
> ing at twice the general rate.[4]

Urban priority areas

This is not so in Britain. The recent story here is one of decline. 'London in Victorian times was the leading city of the world but it had fallen to fourth place in the population league by 1975 and will be below twenty-five by the end of the century.'[5] London's population is falling. People have been moving out to the suburbs and new towns. Others have been decanted from our cities by the wholesale rehousing policies of the 1950s and 60s. UPAs, both inner and outer, consist of communities of the left-behind, suffering from 'economic decline, physical decay and social disintegration'. They constitute 'a different Britain, whose people are prevented from entering fully into the mainstream of the normal life of the nation'.[6]

The Department of the Environment uses six indicators of deprivation for purposes of government policy and resource allocation:

1. Unemployment
2. Old people living alone
3. Single-parent families
4. Ethnicity: proportion in households with New Commonwealth or Pakistan-born heads
5. Overcrowding of homes
6. Homes lacking basic amenities.

It is a deplorable comment on the society in which we live that ethnic origins are used to indicate deprivation.

But members of these minority ethnic groups (4 per cent of the population) are not evenly scattered throughout the land. They are heavily concentrated in some conurbations, in the UPAs, in poorly paid jobs, bad housing and unemployment. They are people who carry a disproportionate share of the burden of adapting to the recent recession and industrial reorganisation in Britain.[7]

Faith in the City concludes:

> The nature of the inequality which burdens the UPAs can be
> elaborated in many different ways. UPAs shelter dispropor-
> tionate numbers of vulnerable people: the unemployed, the
> unskilled, the uneducated, the sick, the old and the disadvan-
> taged minority ethinic groups. They are places which suffer
> conspicuously from low income, dependence on state bureauc-
> racies and social security, ill health, crime, family breakdown
> and homelessness. The sombre statistics of all these conditions
> provide the details of the map of inequality.[8]

Economic decline has been concentrated in UPAs.
Whereas some areas have been losing their working population since the 1920s and 30s, migration out of the inner
city has been a marked feature since the 1960s. 'It is part of
the gradual reduction of the urban working class which is
one of the transformations of twentieth-century Britain.'[9]
This is in contrast to the nineteenth century, which experienced 'an urban working class rapidly coming to numerical
domination of the nation...as unfamiliar to church mission
as it was threatening to secular authority'.[10]

Since 1960 Greater London has lost 50 per cent of manufacturing jobs; 40 per cent have disappeared in other conurbations. It is the unskilled, the unqualified and those ra-
cially discriminated against who lose out, and younger
people are more vulnerable.

Faith in the City also notes, 'to describe UPAs is to write
of squalor and dilapidation. Grey walls, littered streets,
boarded up windows, graffiti, demolition and debris are the
drearily standard features of the districts and parishes with
which we are concerned.'[11] This physical decay is matched
with social disintegration.

> According to the British Crime Survey, robbery victims are
> more likely to live in the inner city, and burglary risk in the
> inner city is double that of the rest of the conurbation and five

times that of the areas outside the conurbations.[12]

The report summarises the situation.

> Poverty reflects the structural inequality of the nation, and the UPAs reveal it in its most intractable forms. The city remains part magnet to the disadvantaged newcomer, part prison to the unskilled, the disabled and the dispirited, part springboard for the ambitious and vigorous who find escape to the suburbs and part protection for enclaves of affluence.[13]

This, then, is the context in which the congregations and fellowships featured in subsequent chapters are called to embody and share with others the experience and hope of God's justice, *shalom* and joy in the Holy Spirit, which are the marks of his kingdom.

Struggle and failure

The story of the church in modern industrial cities is one of heroic failure. This is in contrast to the early church when most congregations were planted and thrived in cities throughout the Roman Empire.

> The city…was the place where new civilisation could be experienced, where novelties would first be encountered. It was the place where, if anywhere, change could be met and even sought out. It was where the Empire was and where the future began. To become a city dweller meant to be caught up in a movement … the tides of migration, the risky travel of the merchant, and even the irregular movement of manners, attitudes and status.[14]

The world of Paul and those first apostolic church planters was thus an urban one.

The churches in Britain were overwhelmed by the rapid growth of the industrial cities. The Church of England, with 1,000 years of experience in parish ministry in a rural civilisation, suffered most; but, because it retained the ideal of 'the parish', it kept on the ground a presence which it still has. There has, however, been no sustained people movement among working-class people in large cities since the onset of the Industrial Revolution. London already had notable problems in Whitefield's and Wesley's time. The early Salvationists and Pentecostalists flourished among working people, as had the Primitive Methodists, but each contributed strongly to the upward and outward mobility of the confident which has characterised the last 200 years. These movements, not sustained beyond the third generation, were outside the established existing denominations of their day. Today the fastest growing churches in the inner cities are the indigenous independent black-led churches.

The Roman Catholic Church, also outside the English religious establishment, has a strong base in the cities.

> Its English history after the Industrial Revolution is quite different (from the mainstream Protestant denominations), because of the influence from the mid-nineteenth century onwards of large migrations from Ireland to many English cities. For many of these migrants from Ireland…Roman Catholicism seemed to be in tune with Irish nationalism and to be marked by a pastoral presence among the poor.[15]

This role in providing cultural identity—repeated for example among Polish Catholics in Chicago—is in contrast to the story of Catholicism on the European continent.

In the later twentieth century 'secularisation—the process whereby religious thinking, practice and institutions lose social significance—has now permeated all sections of society.'[16] Church-going has declined. According to the 1902–03 census of church attendance in London, an average of 4 per cent attended Anglican services in the poorest districts. Research commissioned specially for *Faith in the City* put Anglican church-going in UPAs at 0.85 per cent. It further showed 'middle-class over-representation and working-class under-representation in the congregation and on the PCC...'[17] Other mainline Protestant denominations show a similar tendency; so do many newer house churches, where these exist in the inner city. Some fifty or so congregations have closed since 1945 in the East End of London.[18] The exceptions again are the black-led churches and Roman Catholic congregations.

In contrast to outer estates, inner-city areas are often varied and cosmopolitan. There is evidence that pluralist areas need pluralist forms of the church.[19]

City missions, the settlements, the orders, the societies and other agencies remain at work in inner-city areas. Many have their roots in Anglo-Catholic and evangelical revival movements during the second half of Victoria's reign. Some have adapted with varied success to the vast changes in the inner city. Others remain as shrinking reminders of heroic and costly efforts to redeem the inner city. Church buildings abound in the older UPAs, many the product of the enormous efforts and vision of Victorian Christians.

> It was claimed in 1888 that the Church of England had collected in voluntary contributions £80,500,000 in the years 1860–1885. £35 million of this was spent on church building programmes. The Free Churches spent even more in those years on buildings. The Baptists founded more churches in London in the 1860s than at any other time.[20]

A hundred years later most of these buildings stick out like proverbial sore thumbs, conveying powerfully the message that Christianity is out of date, crumbling and decaying. The wholesale redevelopment of our inner cities has left us with expensive monuments to irrelevance, needing money, time, skill and creative energy to transform into useful plant for effective mission. When prime sites are sold off, all too often churches relocate in the suburbs where church adherence and funding is stronger, thereby aligning traditional Christianity with 'white fright and flight' from the inner area.

Surveys of folk religion (sometimes called implicit religion) show a widespread residual belief in God.

> The British people are by a great majority a believing people, to the extent that some 70 per cent of the population claim belief in God or in some sort of supernatural being. But the moment one goes on to ask, What sort of God?, wide variations occur often related to locality, age, class, education and personal experiences, and not always compatible even when held by the same individual.[21]

> In working-class areas...there is often a strong resistance to any form of organised meeting or regular commitment, and common belief will be found almost invariably outside the church.[22]

Religion is strongly present in a number of inner-city areas. Temples and mosques have replaced synagogues as the Jewish communities have become upwardly mobile and moved to suburbs. 'The great majority of all adherents of other faiths in this country are of Asian origin, most of whom are from the Indian subcontinent. They form not just a religious, but an ethnic community.'[23] Mission in a multi-faith context is a new challenge, dealt with historically through overseas missionary societies. Home churches have been overtaken by events.

All this makes up a formidable—sometimes crushing—historical, economic and religious context for the UPA church. It raises acutely for all churches the question posed for Anglicans in *Faith in the City*.

> Where deep divisions in culture and language exist between different sections of society, a clergy drawn mainly from one section (in the case of England, the middle class) is likely to have serious difficulties in communicating with members of other social groups. In a society where class divisions run so deeply, any institution which attempts to identify itself simultaneously with both the privileged and the depressed faces a

task that is so formidable that it will tend to side with one or the other.[24]

Formidable agenda

The churches featured in the following chapters have to grapple with their particular UPA context while being saddled with the historical legacy—good, bad and indifferent—bequeathed by past generations of Christians. When we face the combined effects of these factors, the wonder is that live and effective congregations *are* present in UPAs! These churches are each a gospel sign. The visits in 1984, 1985 and 1987 of Dr Raymond Bakke—Lausanne consultant on the evangelisation of large cities and author of *The Urban Christian*—unearthed a common agenda for UPA churches. This agenda is shared by those similarly placed in other countries, particularly in the Protestant industrialised West, and—whether consciously or not—it is the agenda of the ten contributors and their churches in this volume. I have expressed this agenda in terms of questions that will, I hope, stir us into action and concern.

What is the church?

Is it the institution or the people—or both? Older churches tend to be dominated by institutional maintenance, the preservation and transmission of 'the tradition'. This is so as much in the Free Churches as among Anglicans, Catholics and Orthodox. Which people? Those who have faithfully preserved the churches' presence, or incomers to the community, or the ordinary people of the neighbourhood? Whose culture predominates? Is a multi-cultural congregation possible? If so, how? The Church at the Centre in Skelmersdale is one church facing these questions, as is Plaistow Christian Fellowship.

How is the local leadership best developed?

The professional clergy and paid ministry dominates in all the traditions except at present the black-led churches and some of the newer house churches. 'For the most part ministers in the black-led churches, both men and women, have to earn their own living and carry out their preaching and pastoral work in their spare time.'[25]

Faith in the City makes a strong case for a serious and sustained effort to develop, in Anglican terms, a local non-stipendiary ministry. This involves local selection, training, recognition and appointment. Training should be practical, earthed in the situation and not assessed by academic criteria. A revolution is also needed in the training of the paid professionals if such are to work effectively in partnership with local leadership.[26] Most churches in this volume have, like the Plaistow Christian Fellowship and the Bonneville Centre in Clapham, worked specifically to train local leaders for ministry.

How is the old core renewed?

The effect of decline is to drive the faithful remnant to hold on, at all costs, to what has been received from the past. The less secure people feel, the less they are able to cope with change. New life breathed into the old by God's Spirit can result in church resurrection. John Holden at Aston and Chris Burch at St Agnes, Burmantofts, have both made this discovery. Incomers who are prepared to commit themselves on a long-term basis to the church and the local community are another means of renewal.[27]

How is diversity to be handled?

Inner-city UPAs, in contrast to outer estates, are varied. Within the general community there is a wide variety of smaller communities, interest groups and client groups, for example single-parent families, single elderly living alone, young unemployed, factory workers, sports and social clubs, ethnic networks. This diversity raises questions about resources and priorities. We can only do so much. Where do we put our effort? Again, both the Ecumenical Church at the Centre and Plaistow Christian Fellowship have wrestled with diversity and triumphed by the love and power of God.

How do ethnic churches and traditional churches relate to each other?

Leaders of the independent black-led churches, in evidence to the Archbishop's Commission, asked to be regarded as equals and treated as such.[28] They sought 'credit where credit is due'—partnership, not patronage. Black-led churches are in fact the fastest growing churches in Britain's inner cities; they deserve a book of their own. Ethnic churches preserve and enhance cultural identity. What shape then should the church take in a multi-cultural situation? Les Ball and Chris Idle of Limehouse in London begin to ask this very question, and John Holden writes in detail of the welding of black and white in Aston.

What are the pastoral priorities?

The urgent and deep-seated needs within the congregation conflict with demands from those outside. In areas where health and social services are being cut back, the church and its leadership are one of the few dwindling sources of help. To whom do we respond and why? How should we do so? In her chapter about the parish of Bestwood, Nottingham, Mavis Bexon shows vividly the implications and cost of the Christian response to deprivation. Philip Scanlan of St Peter's, Cardiff, has a similar story to tell.

How is cross-cultural evangelism to be undertaken?

This issue is acutely faced by any incomer, particularly those whose class background, education and status as a teacher, social worker, manager, civil servant or minister make them outsiders—one of 'them', not one of 'us'. How do we cross ethnic boundaries, particularly where religion, culture, family and identity belong together, as in Hindu and Sikh communities and Protestant and Catholic communities in Belfast? What about other subcultures such as the gang of teenagers or the band of football supporters? How is the gospel to take root in these different worlds in which people feel safe and to which they belong? Graham Bewley in his chapter on St John's, Park, in Sheffield, has wrestled beside his lay leaders with this thorny question, as has Jim Rea at the East Belfast Mission.

How is the competitiveness of the churches to be overcome?

Each congregation can appear to be holding the local franchise for a national denomination, fighting for its share of a dwindling market. Individual churches defend their share! Churches need to recognise that each is gifted by the Spirit and able to offer that gift to the others. No one fellowship can reach, penetrate, serve and teach the complicated interlocking networks of an inner-city area. As each recognises the others' calling, churches can learn to work in complementary fashion. Plaistow Christian Fellowship and Top Valley, to give two examples, have

consciously worked to avoid the 'fiefdom'
local churches.

How is the discouragement of church leadership to ...ealt with?

In tough situations ministerial burn-out is not uncommon.
Faith in the City reports that it is twice as high as
elsewhere.[29] Living and working in areas where the social
needs and pressures are at least twice as high as elsewhere
takes its toll. Envy of others can develop either on one's
own patch or beyond it. Raising a family, the education of
children, taking holidays when empty houses are readily
burgled—all produce anxiety. Frustration with those in authority in the church who don't understand and won't listen
to our story, no means to offload and talk openly, weariness
with incessant demands, the sense of being the forgotten
army—all these affect the morale and well-being of those—
lay and professional—called to lead God's people. Chris
Idle is frank about some of the discouragements he and his
family have faced in this way—but equally frank about the
joys of serving Christ in the inner city. And John Holden of
Aston charts the steady power of prayer in the face of discouragement.

What is the relationship between the spiritual and social in mission and ministry?

How do spirituality and social justice relate? What kind of
spirituality sustains consistent ministry in UPAs?

Worship in the UPAs must emerge out of and reflect local cultures; it will always be the worship of him who is totally other
and is to be found, worshipped and served through the realities
of UPA life. The worship of the church that is part of the UPA
will be the worship of a church that is present in celebration,

confession, compassion and judgement.[30]

Compassionate service as an aspect of worship should be demonstrated and fostered. How? Almost all the contributers to this volume write perceptively of the balancing act involved in making the gospel concrete.

How is fragmentation to be overcome?

Joining hands with other Christians locally takes time and effort. Overstretched people haven't the spare energy to give to co-operative endeavour. Each is fully stretched: building, repairing and maintaining his or her own part of the wall. Skelmersdale would surely echo this statement:

> Ecumenical partnership is a central part of the Christian response to God. Sectarian church life contradicts the calling of the church to be universal, crossing all boundaries of race and class. Faced with the challenge of UPA life we must do together what can in conscience be done together.[31]

How can partnership between suburban and urban congregations be established?

The increasing polarisation between inner city and outer suburb has recreated two nations in Britain. The political map of Britain following the 1987 election shows this with stark clarity. Christians are to be found predominantly in 'comfortable Britain'. The growth of the suburbs has been at the expense of the UPAs. Suburban affluence sustains inner-city impoverishment. The demands of inner-city ministry and mission challenge the consciences, attitudes, values, lifestyles and priorities of suburban Christians and churches. The hard task is to build effective partnership without patronage. This requires a willingness to listen, see, feel, understand and share. It's a two-way process. Suburban and rural Christians have a great deal to learn *from* inner-city Christians. Resources of skill, of people, of money and know-how are needed in the inner city, but they are to be used as local people decide. Reconciliation expressed in practical partnership by churches becomes a sign to the nation of how divided Britain can begin again to be made whole.[32] John Richardson's book *Ten Rural Churches* describes, for example, how one rural Methodist church in Weobley, Herefordshire, twinned with a West Indian church in inner-city Birmingham. The learning that went on was two-way!

How can we deploy and support Christians in structures and institutions?

Christians are called as salt and light to penetrate and permeate the life of the community where God has placed them. Local government, the police, the courts, schools, hospitals, shops, businesses, offices, factories, clubs and voluntary organisations are the sinews of the political, economic, social and cultural life of the area. The biblical vision of God's kingdom restored is of our world once again turned right side up. God's people are together to be his agents of this transformation. Mavis Bexon and Helen Bonnick are two of the contributors who believe in and act on this conviction.

How is the tension between maintenance and mission resolved?

Numerically weak, without adequate resources, having outmoded and inadequate facilities—a church's primary preoccupation can be to keep its act together and its show on the road. Talk of mission increases guilt and induces paralysis. But such concern for internal affairs turns churches into private clubs, the hobby of those who wish to join and use their time and energy in harmless pursuits. Without mission, churches die; Chris Burch and Les Ball make this point quite clearly. The church exists for God's glory and purposes in this world, not for her own ends. Her reason for being is compassionate service to others, showing and telling God's good news centred in Jesus the Messiah.

Life and hope

This is a daunting agenda. Ray Bakke reports that according to the findings from church leaders in consultations held in over one hundred cities on all six continents, the blocks to obedient action come very largely from within the church and not from outside constraints.[33] There are, however, signs of hope.[34] The stories set out in the following chapters are part of this picture. *Ten Growing Churches* and *Ten New Churches* also contain some case histories of UPA congregations.[35]

Evidence submitted to the Archbishop's Commission showed that the lively and effective churches of varied churchmanship and theological persuasions—even if they are small and impoverished—had the following common characteristics:

> Worship rooted in the life of the area, expressed in the local language, reflecting the local culture and lifestyles.
> Team leadership involving local people, and with each believer exercising his or her own gifts in conjunction with others.
> Some outward-reaching project or service however small, in response to needs in, and contributing to the life of, local community.
> Partnership with all local Christians – black and white, in newer churches and older denominations – rooted in a shared commitment to Christ and the neighbourhood.[36]

Look out for these characteristics in the stories that follow!

Great interest has arisen in the base communities or grass-roots churches which have grown up within the Roman Catholic Church in Latin America. There may be 100,000 to 150,000 of these in Brazil alone. Their characteristics have been noted as being—

> gatherings of the poorest and most oppressed, organised into small groups with deep mutual sharing and rooted in the neighbourhood.... Their primary focus is a shared Bible study, using Scripture to reflect on current social issues in the locality and their experiences as a community. The members do not recognise any separation between religion and daily life; they translate their faith into concrete political action. They are usually lay led.... They are deeply committed to the Catholic Church, with a vision of the church which emphasises collective responsibility and fellowship.... Worship and the Sacraments are related to the needs and the experience of individuals and of the community.[37]

By the Spirit, God is planting, renewing, reshaping his church in the inner cities and outer estates of Britain. Churches of the urban poor have come into being around the world. These churches are gospel signs. They speak prophetically to the church at large, particularly to the affluent and powerful. They speak to those in power in church and state who oppress the poor. They are in the vanguard of the evangelisation of the world's cities.

As stories are told, experiences shared, knowledge gained and information exchanged, we are able to understand what is required to plant, sustain and propagate fellowships and congregations of God's people, who embody and extend his kingdom among the hurting, the hidden and the marginalised in our cities. The accounts which follow are offered as an encouragement to those similarly called. Those in comfortable situations have much to learn from them. All are challenged to receive as well as to contribute.

'If you have ears, then, listen to what the Spirit says to the churches' (Rev 3:22).

Notes

[1] The report of the Archbishop of Canterbury's Commission on Urban Priority Areas, *Faith in the City* (Church House Publishing: London, 1985), p iii.

[2] *ibid*, p 3 para 1.1.

[3] Figures produced by UNESCO.

[4] *Faith in the City*, *op cit*, p 3 para 1.1.

[5] *ibid*, p 3 para 1.2.

[6] *ibid*, p 9 para 1.17.

[7] *ibid*, p 10 para 1.20.

[8] *ibid*, p 13 para 1.23.

[9] *ibid*, p 14 para 1.25.

[10] *ibid*, p 5 para 1.6.

[11] *ibid*, p 18 para 1.34.

[12] *ibid*, p 20 para 1.39.

[13] *ibid*, p 25 para 1.50.

[14] Wayne Meeks, *The First Urban Christians* (Yale University Press: New Haven, Connecticut, 1983), p 16.

[15] *Faith in the City*, *op cit*, p 41 para 2.49.

[16] *ibid*, p 31 para 2.19.

[17] *ibid*, p 35 para 2.32.

[18] Colin Marchant, research referred to in David Sheppard, *Built as a City* (Hodder and Stoughton: London, 1974), p 80.

[19] Driscoll and Smith, *West Ham Christians 1984*: *A Summary of the Report to the Archbishop's Commission on Urban Priority Areas* (London ECUM: 1984).

[20] Sheppard, *op cit*, p 113.

[21] *Faith in the City*, *op cit*, p 66 para 3.38.

[22] *ibid*, p 66 para 3.39.

[23] *ibid*, p 61 para 3.27.

[24] *ibid*, p 32 para 2.20.

[25] *ibid*, p 43 para 2.27.

[26] *ibid*, p 67 para 3.40 and p 106ff.

[27] See the account of Ichthus Fellowship in *Ten Growing Churches*.

[28] *Faith in the City*, *op cit*, pp 42 and 43 paras 2.52 to 2.57.

[29] *ibid*, p 133 para 6.95.

[30] *ibid*, p 135 para 6.101.

[31] *ibid*, p 78 para 4.25.

[32] See *Faith in the City*, *op cit*, pp 100–105, for practical suggestions.

[33] See *The Urban Christian* (MARC Europe, 1987).

[34] See Colin Marchant, *Signs of Hope* (Hodder and Stoughton, 1985).

[35] *Ten Growing Churches* and *Ten New Churches* (MARC Europe, 1985 and 1986).

[36] See *Faith in the City*, *op cit*, pp 73–81.

[37] *ibid*, footnote p 80.

Chapter 1

The Church at the Centre

Skelmersdale, Lancs

Norman Winter

When Norman Winter and his wife Cathy first moved from Liverpool to Skelmersdale New Town, they found that although they were 'in the country' geographically, they had in fact come to an urban priority area where the promised land of the ideal new urban centre had not come to pass. Joblessness and closing factories, with consequent discouragement and pressures on family life made 'Skem' seem to many a trap. But through the vision of faithful Christians in the 1960s, the Ecumenical Church at the Centre had combined four denominations—Methodist, URC, Baptist and Anglican—in creating a vibrant Christian community ready to face the challenge. With Bob Andrews, centre administrator, and other ministerial colleagues, Norman served faithfully for seven years among the diverse groups who make up this unusual congregation. The story of the 'Eccy' is one of courage and encouragement for us all.

Though he first believed he was called into overseas mission after university, Norman in fact entered a different mission field: the urban areas of northern England. He now works as a producer for network radio, at the BBC in Manchester. His three children keep him busy, but he finds much-needed recreation in bird-watching, wine- and bread-making.

A week goes by

Tuesday evening The junior-school-aged 'Junior Pilots' have gone home. Some of them we shall see again on Sunday morning, at family worship. Disco music is playing loudly in the hall, competing with the sound of the video in the coffee bar. Pool balls click. There is table-tennis in the dining area, overlooking the hall, and some of the lads, eager to play five-a-side, shout encouragement for the netball practice to end. At the entrance there is still a slight crush as more of the fifty members expected that night come into the youth club.

Norman Edmondson, leader-in-charge, is coaching the younger girls' netball team who, he hopes, will some day have the same success as the main team has already had this year at the Royal Albert Hall, putting Skelmersdale on the map with another trophy at the national Methodist Association of Youth Clubs assembly. Winning at football or netball comes as a boost when only 20 per cent of the town's school-leavers can ever expect a real job. Jean Lunt, part-time leader with Norman over the years, and steward in the church, opens the doors for her latest venture, the computer group. Margaret Blake, the full-time youth worker funded by the local authority, also a Methodist local preacher, is away driving a coach to Finland with another group of teenagers, some from the centre, on an international exchange.

At the same time, half a mile away, members of the church's music group are getting down to practise for next Sunday. Piano, three guitars, flute and a variety of percussion, in changing combinations, with six voices aged fourteen to fifty, all female, prepare for worship:

> Look around you, can you see?
> Times are troubled, people grieve.
> See the violence, feel the hardness;
> All my people, weep with me.[1]

The words ring true, but there is joy and hope for the people of 'the Eccy'—as the centre is popularly known.

Wednesday morning Bob Andrews, centre administrator and United Reformed Church minister, is in his office doing accounts and ready to welcome any visitor. Downstairs, the coffee bar—in place of last night's video and pool—offers a place for a drink and a chat. The local schools are on half-term, so no playgroup meets this morning; there are fewer parents and babies than usual, but one or two of those coming to the 11 o'clock Communion service in the chapel have met there. Derryck Evans, Methodist minister, is available in the vestry before the service begins. As superintendent of the circuit, he gives half his time to the centre and to associated areas of ministry. I arrive to share in the service just as the minibus drives up bringing the first group of elderly people for today's lunch club. Its special tail-lift proves invaluable. The service begins, very informally, but quietly too, with neither of us robed. Today Derryck leads the intercessions, which follow a time in which we all share news of people and problems needing our prayers. We all share the Peace, and I take my place to preside for the rest of the service.

Through the wall comes the sound of volunteers preparing lunches. Two are church members who offer this as their ministry. Upstairs, the busy Workbase offices (sponsored by the Liverpool Industrial Mission and funded by the Manpower Services Commission) are humming with activity. They take up about half the space on the L-shaped upper floor, which looks down on two sides on to the square hall below. While the hall is not in use, Ronnie Lunt, the full-time caretaker (himself among the parish's 40 per cent male adult unemployed before being appointed) takes the chance to get a repair done, helped by a lad on a Community Service Order. Maybe that lad, too, will pick up some of the pride in doing a good job which, with irrepressible Scouse wit, makes Ronnie such a valuable member of the centre team.

Friday afternoon Back in the hall, two youth club sessions, one playgroup, and one old-time dancing session later, Ronnie lays out a hundred or so chairs in a large semicircle, ready for Sunday's Communion service. This weekend there is no booking for Friday night or Saturday; on other weeks it might be a cage-bird show, a blood-donor session, or a wedding. Each week gives the chance to set out chairs in proportion to the number of worshippers expected, and in a layout that enhances the worship. At the centre of the semicircle of chairs stands the Communion table, at floor level, on a rectangular carpet. Behind hangs the large backdrop, in green and yellow and orange and brown, made by members of the congregation. Within a large circle, four smaller circles decorated with symbols of the four evangelists surround a cross. Four Christian denominations: at one around the cross. The wider circle expresses the unity, the wholeness, the meeting of heaven with earth for which the Church at the Centre stands.

Sunday morning Prams going out through the side entrance pass the pensioners coming in. Six families (it's an average month) planning to bring children for baptism have just watched the CPAS 'Stairway' filmstrip, following a service of Thanksgiving and Blessing in the chapel. They have each already received a home visit; the baptisms will take place at the family service a fortnight from now. The pensioners have been picked up by minibus, most of them from areas of sheltered housing, but their age group will be a minority in the main family Communion just about to start. A cassette tape of worship songs plays over loudspeakers as folk move from the coffee bar into the hall.

The service begins. During the first hymn a trickle of

latecomers brings the congregation up to the hundred mark. At the back, on the playmat, four or five under-threes are playing with soft toys. The hymn finishes and twenty or so older children go off to other parts of the building for their 'Voyage' groups. This month's theme is peace. For the adults, the service has quite a traditional format; this is one of the weeks when the visitor can tell which bit is the sermon, though next week there may be an acted Bible story, or a breaking into small groups for discussion. The sermon is taken by one of the lay preachers (all women), a minister presides at the Communion, and others from the congregation lead prayers and read.

The children return for the sharing of the Peace, holding hands with the minister, then joining in the mêlée of handshakes and hugs, while the paper doves they have made in their groups as symbols of peace are shown around. To receive Communion, room is made for everyone to fit in the large circle formed around the table, a circle again expressing wholeness and belonging. The minister and the others helping with bread and cup receive last. The service ends with a resounding sense of commitment:

> Forgive us, Father; hear our prayer.
> We would walk with you anywhere,
> through your suff'ring, with forgiveness,
> take your life into the world.[2]

'Into the world'—but not immediately. Tea and cups of squash are served in the coffee bar, while we catch up on news and hope that newcomers find friends. We sing an impromptu 'Happy Birthday' for one of our members. Missing out on the chat, a small group of willing helpers returns to the hall, clearing away the chairs and other furniture for the start of another week.

The Promised Land

The Lancashire village of Skelmersdale grew to a population of around 6,000 at the end of the nineteenth century, when coal mining was at its peak. By the 1930s, most of its mines were closed, the seams too narrow and dangerous to work. Ten miles to the east, inland, Orwell chronicled the impact of depression in *The Road to Wigan Pier*, while fifteen miles to the south-west gangs of Liverpool dockers used to wait each day in the hope of being picked out for work.

The year 1963 saw the closure of the branch-line which linked Skelmersdale to Ormskirk, and thence to Liverpool. In 1964 Skelmersdale, its neighbouring village of Up Holland, and the two-mile square area of farmland in between, were designated a New Town. Liverpool's drastic demolition programme for inner-city slum housing had already moved tens of thousands of families to an outer ring of housing estates, and the development of Skelmersdale represented a leap beyond that outer ring into the green and pleasant land beyond.

A population of 80,000 was projected. Since it was hoped that almost everyone who lived in the town would work in it too, major areas of land were allocated for industrial development. A grand system of dual carriageways and roundabouts was constructed to carry the expected traffic, as well as a motorway link to the M6, just four miles away. These were the days of cheap oil and of high demand for skilled manual labour. The housing was to be developed as a fifty-fifty blend of private and rented, using the latest building techniques and experimental planning ideas. A valley area and the hillside rising to the east were designated as parkland. Tree-lined cloughs (small streams running off that main slope) were integrated into the landscaping programme and retained, while new shrubs and saplings were planted by the hundred thousand.

The town was also to become as self-sufficient as possible, so three major phases of development were planned for the central shopping area, as well as provision of a hospital. The people began to arrive, and found this whole vision in the process of construction around them. The majority came from Merseyside, but others came from all over Britain. Of course Christians were among them.

In 1964, just as Skelmersdale New Town began to grow, a major conference in Nottingham set the agenda for Britain's churches to work towards achieving visible unity. One important step forward was the commitment to set up 'Areas of Ecumenical Experiment'. As the major denominations considered what they were to do in Skelmersdale, they each made their own plans. But it was primarily through the local leadership of existing churches, and through new staff appointed to work in the new housing areas, that a vision for a united Christian congregation took shape. Two estates in particular were on land where there had only been farms before, so no existing church building stood in the way of a totally fresh start.

Eventually, church leaders from the region were invited to take their pick from the various sites designated for church buildings in the town plan. The local ministers' fraternal had by then an alternative plan. Instead of each denomination putting up its own building, they wondered why they should not pool resources and do something together, on a grander sale, adjacent to the central shopping centre. The idea took shape, and a site was allocated. The partner churches were the Church of England, the Methodist Church, the Congregational Union and the Presbyterian Church (to be united in 1972 in the United Reformed Church), and the Baptist Union. Further sympathetic support from the Roman Catholic archdiocese came in the form of a generous donation.

A nucleus of the future congregation began to meet in one of the primary schools on the Tanhouse estate. 'Little Jerusalem', the newly arriving Liverpudlians called it because there were so many flat roofs on the hillside. Ministers from each sponsoring denomination and a committed core of laypeople who had already been church members elsewhere joined with others who were drawn to this new expression of Christian unity.

These were exciting days, as the United Congregation

(so the new church called itself) explored uncharted waters. The old wineskins of the denominations had enough flexibility to contain the new wine of local unity. But much of the pioneering energy had to be generated on the spot, rather than from on high. For instance, a form of welcoming for new Christians into the church's fellowship had to be devised, including believer's baptism and confirmation by both a local Free Church minister and an Anglican bishop, in one form of service acceptable to everyone. All this fostered among the membership a strong conviction of the need to take responsibility in the shaping of the church's life; this conviction has been a strength ever since.

Egypt revisited

Around 1970, the future looked rosy. Factories even competed with each other for workers. That those days ever happened seems almost unbelievable for those of us who have moved into the town more recently. Many of the events of the 1930s have happened all over again, and with less hope of recovery.

Two very large factories closed, with the loss of over 1,000 jobs each. Many other smaller firms, having satisfied the conditions of the subsidies which had drawn them to Skelmersdale in the first place, shut up shop, moved their machinery elsewhere, and left an ever-lengthening dole queue behind. Some workers were lucky, finding other work locally. Others moved away. Before ever reaching its original vision, Skelmersdale was becoming a community of the left-behind. The intended population was cut from 80,000 to just over 40,000. The balance of housing became heavily weighted to the rented sector, a fact made worse by national government's insistence on high density housing of experimental design. Only the first phase out of three for the central shopping area was completed. Just half of those in employment worked in the town. The date promised for a hospital never came nearer than ten years away and sadly remains so. The main continuing attraction of the town is ironically a symptom of the failure of the vision: housing is much more readily available in Skelmersdale, both rented and private, than in Liverpool or the surrounding Lancashire or Merseyside towns. For many, the town has become a trap.

A family from Liverpool is torn two ways. Skem (the Liverpudlians seldom give it its full Lancashire name) offers a house and space. In return, Gran is an expensive bus-ride away. There is even less chance of getting a job than back in Liverpool. Even the fringe benefits of inner-city life—ready access to shops and to hospitals—aren't there. For those born and bred in the city but now living on state benefits or low pay, this is almost a different kind of poverty—a rural poverty.

The experience sorts out the adaptable. Some survive well, even with style. But for many the all-too-familiar features of inner-city poverty have been reproduced in the country: a breakdown of hope, of self-respect, and a collapse of the old skills of homemaking, of the values of family life, and the ability to make community out of adversity.

Although so much has gone wrong or turned sour, it must be part of the providence of God that what the churches did in the boom years has continued and gone from strength to strength. By 1971 the United Congregation was seeking the way to live out its new-found unity in service and mission. Much of the work was done by Bob Andrews, then the Presbyterian minister in the new ecumenical team, who himself had moved from Liverpool after his first ministerial appointment. (His administrative gifts continue to be used up until today, though as minister he now represents the United Reformed Church and the Baptist Union.) The church then decided to build a community centre which would serve the town every day of the week; the congregation was to be called 'The Church at the Centre'. When the foundation stone of the ecumenical centre came to be laid in 1972, it bore the inscription 'Jesus Christ himself is the foundation stone'. The church was the people in all their diversity; they were Christ's people, and he was central to all that the building stood for.

'It will take a generation for the town to understand it,' predicted the architect, and he was right. Some critics have said that it was asking too much for people, uprooted in every way from their familiar surroundings, to come to terms with a church they could not recognise. We still get the comment, 'It's not a real church'. But many find it refreshing that here is a church that does not just talk about unity but lives it out, even if the word 'ecumenical' gets pronounced 'economical' (tell our treasurer that!) or shortened to the affectionate 'Eccy'.

The final social survey of the town, completed in 1983 before the winding up of the Development Corporation in 1984, revealed that 3,000 or more people claimed to have used the ecumenical centre at least once in the previous year. Built to be of service at a time of relative prosperity, the centre continues to serve, but in changing ways. The original emphases on the very young (the playgroup), the teenagers (youth club), and on the elderly (lunch club and day centre), have all continued. But lately much more provision has been made for the needs unemployment brings—from accommodation for Manpower Services Schemes to running an emergency food store. Nursery accommodation has been offered over the years to organisations which have grown up and moved out, such as the Citizens' Advice Bureau and Marriage Guidance.

Christ is our Rock

'Jesus Christ himself is the foundation stone,' reads the foundation stone of the centre. Taken in its context (Ephesians 2), it is a pointer to the way in which our church sees its life and mission. Paul writes about the reconciling work of Christ, which has brought Jew and Gentile into union with God, and—in a new humanity—with each other. Christ is the foundation of a building *project*, not a completed building. The church in each place, whether it be Skelmersdale or Ephesus, is a section of the construction site of a temple where God dwells.

Having a completed building can tempt a church into thinking in static ways about its life. In Skelmersdale we hope that we retain that sense of the church being under construction. That sense of the dynamic, the growing, the emerging structure is also there when we follow the Old Testament echo of Christ the Foundation Stone, and find Christ the rock, the place of refreshment in a desert pilgrimage. In the previous two section headings, writing about the hopes pinned on Skelmersdale New Town, and the collapse of that hope, I very consciously chose images of the Promised Land and of slavery in Egypt. The life of the church is 'between the times', a sign of God's presence in the pilgrimage in hope across a desert.

It is not mainly to the Exodus story, however, that the Church at the Centre has turned in its own pilgrimage (although it is here that many Christian communities among the poor find meaning and identity). Three other 'models' or understandings of our life as a church have been of particular importance: the servant, the people of God and the family of God.

The servant

'The Son of man did not come to be served; he came to serve...' (Mk 10:45). A determining factor in the design chosen for the ecumenical centre was the decision that it should enable the church to be a servant within the local community. The church has no answers unless it listens first to the world's questions. Skelmersdale—with the pooling of resources by different denominations—gave an opportunity to embody that agenda. This remains a guiding principle in much of what we do. There has been much debate in recent years about the relationship of social concern to evangelism. In an important series of house groups and congregational meetings in 1982, which helped set policy for a period following, we used the title 'Restoring the Cutting Edge'. The basis of this was an illustration used by David Watson, comparing the church to a pair of scissors: the handles, exercising the force to make them work, represent worship; the pivot, holding the scissors together, is fellowship; and the twin cutting edges, which need each other, are mission in both word and deed.

We still have much to learn about putting word and deed together. But from the start, we have seen the 'deed' of social concern as full, valid and obedient Christian service, even when the connection to 'word' has not been clear. We have sustained our playgroup, youth club, and care for the elderly as worth doing in their own right. We have been glad when members of the congregation have been the leaders and helpers, because this makes it clear that these things are done in Christ's name, but church leadership has not always proved possible. We believe that actions in fact speak louder than words in an urban culture.

We have grown towards a fuller realisation that the servant-church is to be modelled on Jesus as the Servant of the Lord. In him the agenda of the world and of the Father met, and the same Spirit who was in him is promised to us. Although we have stepped rather falteringly in this direction, we are trying to develop our ministries of prayer for healing, and prayer for peace and justice as complements to our activism.

During the 'Restoring the Cutting Edge' series, one of the groups came forward with a picture which they thought showed what was going on in our life: a tree, with plenty of branches and leaves showing above ground, but with only shallow roots below. If we were to be modelled on Christ the Servant, we were to be rooted, as he was, in a close relationship with God. We took steps to develop a pastoral team, and to strengthen the life of fellowship groups. More recently, we have held a further programme of groups and congregational meetings called 'Looking for Growth', to review the past four years, to take a fresh and realistic look at the make-up and needs of our parish, and to plan for the future.

The people of God

'We commit ourselves...to join hands with all who own Jesus as Lord in making real among urban people the new community of righteousness, peace and joy to which the Holy Spirit is calling us all.'[3] Joining hands with fellow-Christians is not as easy as it ought to be. Yet Christ prayed for his disciples, and for those who would come to faith through their witness, that unity and mission would go together (Jn 17). Unity and mission belong together; a gospel about reconciliation cannot truly be expressed when Christians themselves remain unreconciled.

The achievement of unity between Christian denominations has proved a minefield and has probably contributed a lot to people opting into 'non-denominational' churches. The way we have followed in Skelmersdale is to tackle the hard business of expressing at the local level as much unity as is possible between the four mainstream denominations of which we are part. Being both urban and ecumenical has put a certain strain on us.

Firstly, even having achieved a degree of unity in congregational life, worship and ministry that has made us a bit of a goldfish bowl to be looked into and admired but also scrutinised, we are all too conscious of the need to build that unity further. Also in our geographical parish are an Assemblies of God congregation and two Roman Catholic congregations who meet in schools. We see the need to develop our life alongside theirs so that the total of what we offer more fully expresses God's will for his people here. Our Lent '86 groups, part of the Inter-Church Process 'Not Strangers but Pilgrims', helped us on that front. Both locally and nationally that pilgrimage is leading to a greater commitment to partnership.

Secondly, we are quite sure that it was right for our denominations to work together in Skelmersdale; anything less than a team ministry, united worship and shared mission would have sold the gospel short. However, the internal regulations of the denominations seem more geared to uniting than to extending. It is up to us to be faithful within the particular calling God has given to us, while others are faithful to theirs. In particular we are conscious that, in urban culture, congregational size tends to get stuck at the level where all the regular members can expect to know each other. Numerical growth does not happen beyond that point unless a strong sense of belonging, in other ways, can overcome the feelings of anonymity and loss brought on by growth. We have not yet found an answer. Growth from 67 to over 100 on the membership roll, and from 97 to 117 in family worship average attendance in the period 1978 to 1986 is an indication that if an answer were found we might grow significantly.

Thirdly, while we are totally committed to being ecumenical, we do not always find that ecumenical patterns of practice help our calling to urban mission. Services vary substantially from one week to another and quite often rely at least in part on printed orders. This does not help in establishing a pattern people can memorise, although those who like variety enjoy it. There are quite a few committees, an ecumenical jargon, and four sets of denominational jargons to go with all that. This is something of a deterrent to local people with no church background playing a full part in leadership, though again some have taken to it and become confident in such settings. We believe we have learnt at the very least that, besides the importance of partnership between different denominations, the most important partnership is the partnership of the whole membership, which happens through regular church meetings and a hard-working church council.

The family of God

'God, make us your family' is one of our favourites when it comes to singing our theology! Jesus welcomed children to sit on his knee, and so should we. This is one of the matters that causes debate in most parish churches (and even more in ours, being Baptist as well). We have tried to express that welcome. We meet around eighty families each year wishing to bring children for baptism. All receive a home visit and an invitation to a Thanksgiving and Blessing service, followed by the 'Stairway' filmstrip. We encourage the parents to think about the option of leaving children to grow up to choose baptism in their own time, but most want to continue with their request for infant baptism. If so, we ask them to come to family worship to see the church family first, before bringing their children for baptism into it. The baptisms themselves always take place at the main service. In this way we combine thoughtful preparation with a welcoming, personalised and non-judgemental attitude. Most families are grateful for this, and although fewer than one family in ten ever respond even over a short period by joining the congregation, it has been the biggest single factor in numerical growth.

The welcome for children is genuine. For a while at least, the under-fives have been the largest single grouping within any five-year age spread in the congregation. Four years ago we introduced the playmat at the back of the hall to help parents stay within the worship, but give toddlers room to move around. We have always tried to run family worship for the whole family, with worship together and teaching usually separate. We try to make the children feel very much a part of things when all the ages are together;

we see this as specially important in a setting where great hopes are pinned on the future through the children, as adults are going through hard times in the present.

Being the family of God is not just about the place of children, though the inclusion given to children can be a measure of the genuineness of our claim to be a Christian community. But the family is also the place where there should be honesty (which sometimes means disagreements) and acceptance of each other's weaknesses—far though that is from the family image presented in a cornflakes advert! The family should be a place where we know we are loved, where brothers and sisters convince us of our worth. (When we used the Post Green Community material 'Growing Together in God's Family', we discovered that many of the congregation found the picture of God as Father very unhelpful, so bad were their own family memories; but the picture of Jesus as brother, and of fellow-Christians as brothers and sisters, was very much valued.) The family is also where we do not have to be totally self-sufficient but can be in partnership. This is even more true in a culture which has been built on the extended family. The church family is especially a help to single parents, bringing up children on their own, which includes about one-third of our regular families at present. Church outings from Skelmersdale have brought alive for us the story of Jesus not being missed all day on the pilgrimage home from Jerusalem! Sharing the care of children may have its worrying moments; at its best it is a real relief.

A postscript on membership

The report on the Archbishop's Commission on Urban Priority Areas, *Faith in the City*, said that churches in urban priority areas should become 'local, outward-looking, and participating churches; they must have a clear ecumenical bias'.[4] The ecumenical centre has brought together, in ecumenical partnership, the Church of England, with its emphasis on being local; and the Free Churches, with their emphasis on being outward-looking and participating. Only about one-quarter of our households in membership at present comes from outside our geographical parish, a majority of these having Free Church background. This is understandable as we are also, for instance, the only Baptist church in the town. It has helped root the Free Church witness in a commitment to a locality—the parish.

Culturally (and this can only be an approximation), about one-third of the church membership are middle class, two-thirds working class. In an 80 per cent working-class neighbourhood, that shows something of a middle-class bias, but it also shows in those individuals a commitment to the local church and its mission. Different parts of the congregation are not always on each other's wavelength, because their cultural backgrounds are so different. It is easy for hurts to be caused unintentionally. But one positive factor that has brought people together despite their differences has been the shared experience of all being newcomers to a new environment.

The fact that our average Sunday attendance of 125 only represents just 1 per cent of the parish population can depress us. One can walk past a hundred houses before coming to a church household. Yet that 125, when gathered, can offer encouragement. So much achieved, so much to do!

In the geographical spread of the membership, there is perhaps an indication that we are following in Jesus' own bias to the poor. There is a band of private housing along one edge of the parish. Proportionately fewer people worship with us from that area than from the rest of the parish, which is mainly rented housing. Such a spread is very unusual in a church in Britain.

There is still a high degree of mobility in the town, as people move in and out, and from one size of council house to another as children are born. That mobility is naturally reflected in the church membership roll. In one recent year there was a 25 per cent change in the membership in twelve months. There is more loss by transfer than growth by transfer, so building a congregation is a bit like trying to go up the down escalator.

A most heartening feature of the membership is the fact that the age-profile of the congregation quite accurately corresponds with the age-profile of the parish population. The peaks are in the age-ranges of children and parents; the profile tails off through middle age to the elderly. It indicates that the church is 'in touch'. Certainly the birth of three children in our own family, the first only a month after we moved to Skelmersdale, has kept our feet on the ground and has been a major point of contact with many people around.

Football, anyone?

This, then, is the very different kind of church which the people of Skelmersdale are coming to look upon as normal. As one Skelmersdale child asked his teacher when being shown around a village church in Yorkshire, while on a school holiday: 'How do they put these chairs away when they want to play football?'

Notes

[1] Jodi Page Clark, *Kyrie Eleison* (Celebration Services (International) Ltd, 1976). Quoted with kind permission of Thankyou Music.

[2] *ibid*.

[3] Extract from the *ECUM Manifesto* (Evangelical Coalition for Urban Mission: London, 1981).

[4] *Faith in the City* (Church House Publishing: London, 1985), p 74.

Chapter 2

East Belfast Mission

Newtownards Road Methodist Church

Jim Rea

East Belfast Mission, also known as Newtownards Road Methodist Church, is in the centre of what is commonly called 'loyalist East Belfast'. It is situated just a mile from Belfast city centre on the Newtownards Road and is over-looked by the two giant cranes of the Belfast shipyard of Harland and Wolff. It is also overshadowed, though not daunted, by the local presence of paramilitary organisations and political strife.

Despite all the pressures of inner-city life—the marriage breakdown, poverty and unemployment—East Belfast Mission has continued to exalt the name of the Lord Jesus through its ministry to the outcasts of society, to young people and to the homeless. The Rev Jim Rea, author of this chapter, tells us the heartening stories of several of those who have been drawn to Christ through the Mission.

Jim Rea was trained at Edgehill Theological College in Belfast and served after ordination as Superintendent Minister of the Pettigo and Irvinestown Circuit in County Fermanagh.

He has been at the Mission since 1978. He and his wife Carol and family of two girls and a boy enjoy being together; his own interests include sport, especially cricket. He is a free-lance broadcaster, religious advisor and programme presenter with Downtown Radio, part of the IBA network.

Building and rebuilding

The name Ballymacarrett may sound unfamiliar, but you will have heard of the area if you have watched the past eighteen years' television news coverage of events in Northern Ireland. The area generally referred to as 'loyalist East Belfast' is in fact Ballymacarrett. That description is not specific and usually refers to the area around the Belfast shipyard rather than the wider East Belfast which covers as much of suburbia as it does the inner city.

Methodism in one form or another has had a presence in this community for well over 150 years. On the site of the present East Belfast Mission there once stood one of Methodism's great 'cathedrals', destroyed in 1941 by bombing. This church could seat almost 2,000 people and was at one time the largest Methodist church in Ireland.

The destruction of the building took its toll on the congregation, many of whom lived in the suburbs at a distance from the church. During this wartime period some joined churches closer at hand, and a healthy nucleus began to worship in a local Methodist mission hall at Pitt Street. Pitt Street was a Methodist mission hall connected with another East Belfast church at Mountpottinger. As Pitt Street had no morning service the church at Mountpottinger happily accommodated the remaining friends from Newtownards Road, and this continued for a period of eleven years until 1952, when the present building was opened.

This building, which is our present worship centre, is barn-like but bright and comfortable without offering much in the way of architectural beauty. It can accommodate 700 worshippers.

Some influential people within the Methodist Church in Ireland doubted the wisdom of rebuilding the church. They took the view that there was adequate provision already within the area. Those who made the pilgrimage back were the faithful former members, along with some from the mission hall who shared the joy of a new church building. Among those who joined the new church under the leadership of the Revd Tom Kennedy was County Waterford man W J Hosford, now an octogenarian who remains a man of vision and spiritual leadership.

Those early years in the new church building were times of development; however, difficult years lay ahead. The Revd Tom Kyle became minister in 1965 and had to take the church through the most difficult period in its history. The area was decimated by redevelopment. Hundreds of houses came down in a massive movement of population to new housing estates in the suburbs. Such an upheaval would be traumatic for any inner-city congregation, but added to it was the developing sectarian strife on the streets of East Belfast and the fear that comes with it, both driving away any growth potential for the congregation. During these difficult times valiant efforts were made to keep the work going, and only on one occasion was it necessary for a Sunday evening service to be abandoned due to strife in the area.

Hopelessness and hope

The late 1960s and early 1970s were marked by rioting, looting and sectarian killings on the streets of Belfast. Young people roamed the streets aimlessly, often in danger. The church rose to the situation in the provision of a youth centre and in the employment of a full-time youth leader. Night after night Joe Warke and the Revd Trevor

Kennedy brought kids off the streets into a caring Christian atmosphere. It is widely accepted that due to this work many young people were drawn away from sinister forces in the area.

The year 1978 was eventful for me. I then left Irvinestown in the beautiful lake district of County Fermanagh to become minister of Newtownards Road Church. As a native of working-class Belfast I had looked forward to the challenge, but as I began to work in the church I faced the stark realities. The morning congregation of around 120 was made up of many elderly people. It was obvious that the next ten years were crucial. Other mainline denominations in the area were facing serious decline. Churches in this part of East Belfast had a doubtful future. Funerals appeared more popular than baptisms—over the past 10 years I have conducted almost 300.

Despite the decline in church attendance, this community was not a 'no hope area'. New homes were being constructed, and although only one-third of the number of people originally in the area would be there for the future, nevertheless there was much opportunity.

As the new houses were built, families were returning to the area; however, many of these people had little or no contact with the church. They were part of the growing secular society which largely sees the Christian church as a place to administer baptism, marriage and funerals.

Northern Irish people have a mentality summed up in the words of a famous Ulster politician, 'What we have we hold'. Some people in the Newtownards Road congregation wanted to preserve some of the traditions of the past. The trouble was that what the church had in the past could not be preserved in the new community developing around the church. A new vision was needed and an attempt made to discover the will and purpose of God for the future.

Explosions of a different kind

Evangelism Explosion is the title of a book I had read while
living in County Fermanagh. I soon dismissed the concept
as 'typically American', an idea that would not work in Ireland. It was while rearranging my study shelves that this
book came back into my hands. I read it and reflected on an
article written by a Presbyterian minister, the Revd Dr
Brian Kingsmore. It told how Evangelism Explosion had
been successfully used in a new housing estate where he was
ministering. Brian was known to our congregation, having
played football for our Boys' Brigade team, when he was
centre forward with fair ability. I invited him to speak to a
meeting of interested people. As a result I went with John
Watt for training at an Anglican church in Liverpool, where
the Revd John Banner had effectively worked this programme of evangelism. On our return we immediately got
an Evangelism Explosion programme going. Here I should
explain exactly what was involved: Evangelism Explosion
is an on-the-job seventeen-week training course to help
Christians share their personal testimony and make a gospel presentation. Usually two people are trained initially in
an intensive week-long course, and then they teach the programme over seventeen weeks in the local church. Over the
past ten years we have trained around thirty people in this
form of personal evangelism.

At first we called at the homes of regular worshippers
who appeared to be uncommitted, and then at the homes of
fringe members. The trainees were enthusiastic. They observed John and myself sharing the gospel and began
gradually to do it themselves. Christians of long standing
were thrilled to be able to share their experience of Jesus
Christ for the very first time.

Going from home to home we found more interest in the
Christian faith than we first imagined. Even in an area

where fewer than 10 per cent were regular churchgoers, there was an interest in Christian belief. We could only attribute the warm response to a small prayer group who remained back at the church to pray for those out on the doorsteps and in the homes. Soon we could record our first conversion and others were to follow. Margaret, a young woman in contact with a girl called Lilian (who was not directly involved with Evangelism Explosion but whose husband was involved) came to Christ. Her life had revolved around the drinking-clubs of East Belfast. After her conversion Margaret became the first new convert to join in the Evangelism Explosion programme.

During this period church attendance appeared to increase. Services seemed to bring help to those attending. We developed a free form of Methodist worship giving priority to practical expository preaching that dealt with some of the real-life problems affecting people.

Sorrow and certainty

As a backdrop to all of this was the political strife particular to Northern Ireland. Nearby was the headquarters of two of the loyalist paramilitary organisations, the Ulster Defence Association and the Ulster Volunteer Force. Almost every able-bodied man in the area had some links with these groups. Many were deeply involved and would have difficulty in leaving the organisation concerned.

As the church became more community conscious we became more aware of serious social problems in our community. Nearby stood one of the largest drinking-clubs in the British Isles. Alcoholism was a major problem with ninety-five legal bars within a one-mile radius of our church building. Unemployment was on the increase as Harland and Wolff, the major shipbuilders, faced serious decline; once a workforce of around 26,000, they were now reduced to around 4,000. Marriage breakdown was on the increase

and family life in general came under much threat. Unemployment brought inner-city poverty with families
struggling for survival. Many families had incurred serious
debts which they were unable to clear, and these added
severe pressure.

As our members became more socially aware we decided
we should try to do something for those with alcohol problems. We had no idea how to begin and thought that we
should pray about the matter.

A few days later I received a significant phone call. A
member of the congregation informed me that her husband
Tommy was in a psychiatric hospital where he was being
treated for alcoholism. When I visited Tommy I discovered
that an important change was taking place in his life. Although he had made a Christian profession in his earlier
life, Tommy had become an alcoholic through a variety of
circumstances. But this occasion of hospitalisation brought
with it a new commitment to Jesus Christ. Tommy was concerned to help fellow-alcoholics and insisted that on his
return home from hospital he should begin in our local
church context. The idea of helping alcoholics had been
earlier stimulated in my thinking by Arthur Williams, then
pastor of Findlay Memorial Church in Glasgow. Arthur,
himself a recovered alcoholic, had spoken in our church
and had greatly challenged many of us.

In January 1982, along with Tommy and few others, we
set up a Drop-In day centre at our church. I was not as
optimistic as Tommy as to how successful this would be. We
simply provided wholesome food and friendship. Soon it
became the centrepiece of our work and to this day caters
for between 70 and 100 persons every day.

Sandra, Norman and John

During these years God worked in the lives of a number of
people. Sandra, now our Mission secretary, came to our

church one Sunday evening. She had returned from London and felt drawn to attend a church. She came to her first service in Newtownards Road, heard about Jesus and was moved to consider committing her life to him. A few days after this initial contact she became a Christian. Now she works full time in the Mission, offering her excellent gifts in administration.

Norman was a chronic alcoholic. He was contacted by Tommy, who surprised him by being sober. Later Norman attended a local Baptist church where he came to Christ. He also began to help in the mission's ministry to alcoholics.

Things began to develop as we realised the serious unemployment problems of our area. Our centre needed staff, and so through government funding we began to create jobs. This was initially work in our kitchen, cooking simple meals. The Department of Economic Development took an interest in our scheme and encouraged us in its development. With the co-operation of eight other Methodist churches, we now have over twenty people employed on this programme. About eleven work in our Drop-In day centre, and the other twelve or so work out in the community, some doing handiwork for pensioners and visiting people with special needs.

Early in our employment scheme we took on John as a cleaner. He was well known to us and to the area. John was a paramilitary who had spent over four years of his life in prison. He also had serious drinking problems. Part of our ministry was giving jobs to people we thought might be helped by working at our centre. John was seen by the people of our area as an ardent loyalist and supporter of Glentoran Football Club. He was something of a character.

After some weeks of employment John became interested in Christian things. The Holy Spirit began to speak to him in a number of ways. One Saturday evening in February 1984 I received a telephone call and was asked to make contact with John. This conversation later led to his conversion.

Since then John has become actively involved in the work of the Mission, particularly among young people. With others he has developed an existing youth work which is a splendid means of outreach to young people. Every Friday and Saturday around sixty to eighty kids gather and on Sunday evening around thirty to forty attend our evening service.

John is now attending the University of Ulster, studying for a diploma in youth and community work, and our hope is that he may be able to develop full-time youth work with our Mission in the future.

Mission status

The year 1985 was a momentous year for Newtownards Road Methodist Church. After much negotiation and planning, the Methodist Conference allowed this congregation to become a Methodist mission. Our leaders and congregation had begun to see this possibility as the work of the day centre developed. Mission status has given us greater flexibility. It allows us to appeal to the wider public for financial support. It offers us the opportunity to have on our committee people from other churches—people with specific expertise. It allows for the continuity of ministerial leadership and most of all offers the church a concept of openness and 'down to earthness' relevant to our area.

Many in Northern Ireland will remember Saturday 23rd November 1985 as the day of protest when hundreds of thousands of people brought the country to a standstill in protest at the signing of the Anglo-Irish Agreement some days earlier. That very same day was set for the official opening by the president of the Methodist Church in Ireland of the East Belfast Mission. Despite encouragement by the security forces that we should postpone, it was generally felt that we should go ahead. With a certain amount of anxiety we awaited the mid-afternoon starting time, but to our amazement were thrilled to see around 700 people pack our church as a confirmation of the direction we had taken. It was also a historic day for the kingdom of God.

At times it is difficult to understand why our church has grown in the inner city. Two-thirds of our morning congregation of around 270 have joined us in the last 10 years.

Sometimes I am so close to the situation that I don't know why things happen. Undoubtedly there are the convictions and vision of our committed laypeople, open to God's will for the future. People seem to want to come together for prayer and Bible study. Our mid-week group has grown from around a dozen to almost fifty. Together we share concerns commonly felt. The Bible is studied and applied. This group is popular and provides warm fellowship, although strangely we have never developed much support for house groups, which don't seem to catch on in our area.

During my ten years of ministry we have had two lay witness weekends. These are times when members from other churches come to share their personal experience of God. The weekend commences on Friday evening and concludes on Sunday. The lay witness teams conduct rallies, services and house groups. These occasions have brought great renewal to us. At these events we have seen many converted and at our last weekend over twenty members of our youth club made a profession of faith.

On another lay witness occasion two young men, Peter and Edward, were challenged about Christian service. Both these young men are now Methodist ministers, the first to enter the Christian ministry from our congregation in over fifty years.

The intensity of these occasions is not always easy to maintain as it is often the result of a spontaneous outpouring of the Holy Spirit. Nevertheless, each week we try to maintain services of worship that have spontaneity, lay participation and biblical teaching evangelism. Preaching has an important place in the Mission, and an attempt is made to popularise Christian truth and make it relevant to the worshippers.

In 1978 our income was around £10,000 per annum. Now our total income with all grants and public giving amounts to almost £250,000. God continues to provide for our needs. Our ministerial team has been strengthened by the appointment of Helen as pastoral assistant. Seeing the need for further pastoral help we prayed both for the finance and the right person, and this prayer has been answered. The pastoral team now includes our lay pastor George, a former shipyard worker, and Helen our pastoral assistant, along with myself. Together we give regular pastoral support to people with every conceivable need.

Looking to the future

As I write we are contemplating the building of a residential centre for the homeless. We hope this will be completed by 1990 and will provide a place of refuge for many broken people from within our community. Some of us are also looking at ways to provide self-employment for people without jobs with the creation of a small industrial complex. However, we never forget our first call to lead men and women to Jesus Christ. This conviction is shared by all within our congregation: by the old members like Stevie, a well-known character of the Newtownards Road who is heard before he is seen, but has given years of committed service even when things have not been easy; and by the recently converted young and old who have found new hope in Jesus Christ.

Our own community has its own perception of the East Belfast Mission. Some have criticised us, believing we have lost the dignity of a church and have directed too much attention to the social outcasts. Some offer criticism of a leadership that shows openness to everyone regardless of religion or creed.

Our hope is that we please God, that we do his will, that we seek no reward other than giving supreme lordship to Jesus Christ. With Methodist hymn writer Hugh Sherlock we sometimes sing:

> In the streets of every city
> Where the bruised and lonely dwell,
> Let us show the Saviour's pity,
> Let us of His mercy tell.
> In all lands and with all races
> Let us serve, and seek to bring
> All the world to render praises,
> Christ, to thee Redeemer, King.[1]

Note

[1] Quoted from 'Lord, thy church on earth is seeking', hymn 774 in the *New Methodist Hymnbook* (Methodist Publishing House: 1985), with grateful acknowledgements.

Chapter 3

Bonneville Baptist Church
Clapham Park, Lambeth, London

Les Ball

Founded in 1961, Bonneville Baptist was a young, enthusiastic independent church that was nevertheless facing discouragement when Les and Ann Ball first arrived. Formerly a teacher, Les came with energy and vision for a growing church: for new facilities, leadership training and outreach. He and his fellow-leaders—David, Richard and Peter—are committed to three principles in their ministry: reaching up to God, reaching in to God's people and reaching out to the world. The stories he tells in this chapter show exactly how these principles are applied.

Les was trained at the London Bible College and brought his family to Bonneville in 1974. He is a football fan, the proud father of teenagers Stephen and Abigail, and the owner of a well-walked labrador.

The newly built Bonneville Christian Centre stands right on the South Circular trunk road as it winds its way from Clapham Common towards Brixton Hill. Most of this two-mile stretch is bordered by blocks of flats on four large council estates, behind which are found rows of well-kept Victorian terraced streets. Opened at the end of 1986, the modern, light and spacious two-storey building has quickly become a local landmark and source of community pride in an area devoid of focal points. It is also the focus of a growing group of Christians seeking to infiltrate this exciting, multi-cultural neighbourhood for Jesus Christ, and to see his kingdom's rule brought to bear in many lives.

The evidence that this is happening is found on Sundays, when the building throbs with life: young and old, black and white, offer praise to God from the 350-seater worship area. The story of how Jesus Christ has made his mark on this inner-city area—so familiar with wailing sirens, broken windows, hovering helicopters, muggings, vandalism and graffiti—is not one of spectacular success, but rather one of slow, steady growth as a result of faithfulness in prayer and service by a few in the face of great disappointment and discouragement.

Early days

When my wife, Ann, and I were invited to pastor Bonneville Baptist Church, Clapham Park, in 1974, the church was then only thirteen years old. Beginning as a Sunday school in the 1930s, meeting in Bonneville Junior School (which is where our name originates from), a large work grew up under the supervision of Balham Baptist Church. After the war, when changes in local government policy made the hiring of schools difficult, the church members decided to purchase our present site (a bomb site then) and build a hall suitable for young people's work in the Clapham Park area.

In the face of stiff opposition, the church was miraculously able to buy the land and in 1958 a single-storey building was opened, not just for a Sunday school, but also for outreach services to the parents (still under the direction of Balham Baptist). In 1961 sixty-six members covenanted together to form an independent church. The next few years, however, were to test severely that pioneering faith; a succession of ministers came and went, one in very tragic circumstances. When I arrived in September 1974, the fourth minister in twelve years, my wife and I were greeted by a small group of committed members desperately eager to please God, yet battle weary and in need of much encouragement. The setting up of a church office was to become the means God used to do this and the beginning of a whole new era for Bonneville.

We asked the church in November 1974 to join us in a faith project—praying in £250 by the end of December to pay for the plastering and furnishing needed to transform the breeze block vestry into a functional office. Many members confessed afterwards to watching this rather sceptically; certainly we felt as if our faith was on trial, and so it was with great delight that we announced on the last Sunday of the year that the money had come in. The church had turned a corner as people saw something tangible change. As the office came into being, complete with telephone and printing facilities, faith and expectation levels began to rise. We all saw God at work.

While we attended to this groundwork, we also laid other foundation stones. We began to prune the Sunday school, slowly cutting back on the size of the work in an attempt to stop the 'tail wagging the dog', releasing more members for the real challenge of reaching adults. This was not easy, as the Sunday school was still seen as the jewel in Bonneville's crown, and I was often reminded of the words of Jesus, 'Suffer the little children to come unto me'. We avoided confrontation by continuing to support the teachers, yet not actively finding replacements for those who had to retire. I also discouraged the practice of automatically putting teenagers leaving the senior department straight back in as teachers, convincing the church that they needed to grow in their own faith first.

To do this we opened our home on Sunday nights after the evening service for a time of fellowship and 'any questions', Bible study, and prayer for the young people. We were soon bursting at the seams with spiritually hungry youngsters, especially as the Boys' Brigade and Girl Guides flourished under dedicated leaders. It was clear to us there was enormous potential here...but we needed help if it was to be fully realised. This request—for God to increase the number of harvest labourers—was at the top of our prayer list.

Sundays started to become exciting as new folk began to join us, many of them through the Navigators (a group that had influenced our early days as Christians). Disappointing times came, however, during holidays when the new people went back to their homes, for this reminded us again of the real need to raise up *local* people as leaders.

With this in mind, we started a small evangelism training programme in 1975, following my attendance at the first Evangelism Explosion clinic in Britain, at Northwood. On Tuesday and Thursday evening I took two teams (three in a team) into the neighbourhood giving 'on the job' training on how to bring people to Christ in their own homes. We began by visiting fringe members and those who occasionally visited the church. What an education it proved to be, and an insight into where people really were! One Muslim man suddenly asked me, politely but firmly, to leave his house as I was not a true man of God because I had put my Bible (God's holy book) on the floor next to the seat I was sitting on. Another team spent an evening with a West Indian man stretched out on a sofa and wearing only underpants—the worse for drink and with the TV full on—trying to convince him that he was not perfect and that we have all sinned!

As our confidence grew, we began visiting the blocks of flats opposite the church. They had been closed for a number of years awaiting extensive modernisation. As each flat was completed and reopened, we would visit the new tenants with a special 'welcome' pack, giving information about the church and the area. We had many lovely conversations, some eventually leading to professions of faith, of which that of Ron Eastham (a retired London fireman) and Alice Taylor (a housewife) were particularly significant—both of them making quite an impact for Jesus Christ through their own networks of family and friends.

It was during these days of learning how to evangelise an inner-city multi-cultural community that we discovered a vital principle, which still lies at the heart of our outreach today—that we gained our best hearings in the homes we had served in some way. If we had looked after their children in the Sunday school or a youth group, or had been able to help at times of sickness or bereavement, we were welcome visitors. Serving works pave the way for saving faith; the ground has to be loosened first before it can receive the seed. Realising this connection, we began to appreciate our youth organisation in a new way, encouraging its leaders to see their group as a vital part in the overall evangelistic strategy of our church. It also helped my wife and me to look upon our weeks at the Boys' Brigade annual summer camp in a different, more positive light!

One person who exhibited a real gift in evangelism was Heather King, a health visitor, whom we had met at the London Bible College and who had joined us in the church when we first moved. She began working half a day a week for us, helping in pastoral visiting, and was soon invited by the church to become our second full-time worker; the evangelistic and pastoral value of having someone out visiting all the time quickly became apparent. Soon following hers was the appointment of Glenn McWatt as our administrator, to co-ordinate efficiently the now fast-expanding office work. Financial support for Heather and Glenn was helped by the fact that they each lived in a combined household: the one for ladies being next door to the manse, and the men having the use of an empty vicarage.

In 1979 our church membership reached the 100 mark—

an occasion for great rejoicing because since introducing covenanted membership in 1975 we knew God had indeed done a solid work; these 100 were fully committed. Each July we released all members from their commitment and asked them to review during the summer whether or not they still wanted to serve God at Bonneville, and in what capacity. September saw the start of each new church year with a rededication service, when we would covenant together to serve God and support each other in the Lord. This annual event enabled us all to evaluate regularly our spiritual gifts, talents, giving and skills, and made it easier to move unsuited people into more suitable jobs. It also produced a strong financial base (our annual income rose from £4,000 in 1975 to £19,000 in 1980). We still practise this policy, and it is still doing us good (an income in 1986 of £58,000 from our 170 committed members). While the congregation might be larger, it does save a lot of frustration knowing who is committed to the work and can be called upon when needs arise.

This growth in numbers of committed members was matched also by continued, healthy growth in our youth groups, and we began to face tension because of the lack of facilities in our limited buildings. Every evening our halls were in use; our Boys' Brigade hired a nearby school three evenings a week, yet I was reluctant to recommend to the church that we build something larger; I felt strongly our resources should be employed in evangelism rather than tied up in plant.

In 1979 a way round this seemed to open up when a Christian retiring to the country offered us his large five-bedroomed detached house at a reasonable price. Selling the manse enabled us to buy this house and even gave us a surplus to start modernising it. With a large through lounge, we soon transferred all our prayer meetings, church meetings, committee meetings and so on to the new manse, freeing more space for youth activities at the church.

Moving out

The problem of space, however, refused to go away, especially on Sundays, when we often had standing room only. We tried a closed circuit TV relay for a while, but for two years the need to build haunted us, until in November 1981 we made a momentous decision—to begin a faith project on a totally different scale from our first £250 project—that of building a new complex that would finally cost over £600,000 when completed in 1986.

God confirmed this to us, giving several members in November the same verses he had given Ann and me while we were away on sabbatical that summer: 'Make the tent you live in larger; lengthen its ropes and strengthen the pegs!' (Is 54:2). That evening, after the church had decided to build, I shared the story of the provision of meat by air mail (quails!) for the Israelites when, in the desert, they were complaining to Moses about the manna (Num 11). That amazing act of God was for our encouragement, I said —not imagining just how prophetic that was to be. Next morning we had a phone call from a lady whose freezer had broken down. Could we use some joints of meat? What a thrill to distribute two sacks of frozen meat to the deacons and others in the church—God's seal on the previous night's decision; he was going to be our provider as well!

Three of our deacons were appointed the building committee; their job was to liaise with and oversee the architect and contractors. A small finance team was set up to research cash flows and handle the complex financial negotiation. Another small group was invited to meet with me once a week to thank God for every single gift received and to pray for the provision of the remainder. We were led to the biblical story of the multiplication of the fishes and loaves as our guiding financial principle, encouraging all members to give what they could, and then looking to heaven for a miraculous multiplication. This soon started to happen, £50,000 being reached, then £100,000. The prayer team was thrilled and decided it was not right to keep the blessings to themselves, so an early morning Tuesday prayer meeting was started, open to everyone to come and thank God for the gifts received the previous week and to pray for further multiplication.

At the end of 1984 we went out to tender and were soon faced with the possiblity of a contract committing us to a final cost of around £670,000. At that time we had £105,000. We needed God's encouragement to trust him to move ahead. It came in March when we asked God for 100 members to sign a pledge that they would be committed to praying and giving to see the project through.

We got that commitment. Our 'Company of the Committed' gave £20,000 that first weekend in March and pledged themselves to give a further £220,000 over the next four years. The people were believing God and doubting their doubts! The deacons put their houses up for security as well against bank loans; and so, in faith, we signed contracts, and building began in the summer of 1985 for our new two-storey centre on the land next to our original buildings.

News

There was no chance, however, to become obsessed with the new building. We were hearing a new word from God: he wanted a new church to go into the new church! He wanted the leadership and structures to change. Those who had nurtured the young Bonneville now had to loose their grip over the child, now fast maturing, if its growth was not to be restricted.

The implications of this were far-reaching, especially for Ann and me. We divided the fellowship into five geographical areas and appointed a married couple to have pastoral oversight for all the Christians in their area, and to be responsible for developing an evangelistic strategy suitable for their area. These groups began meeting in September 1985: once a month for worship, once a month for evangelism, and twice a month for fellowship. It was a strange feeling seeing others start to pastor the flock and lead them out in evangelism, hearing others talk about the possibility of church planting. We were now actually letting our church go, something for which God had been preparing us for quite a while. It has been exciting to see the developments since then.

We still have a strong team of full-time staff, exercising more and more an enabling type of ministry, but now overseen by four elders, of which I am one. We see our role as to encourage and guide the flocks, not to dominate them. We teach certain principles as vital to please God, but we allow freedom in the actual expression of those principles. Hence, for instance, the evangelism methods actually employed by the group working in the Brixton Hill area will differ greatly from those used, say, in the Streatham Hill area.

Bonneville's leadership principles

The diagram on the next page indicates the principles we are committed to as a leadership.

Reaching up to God's heart

Expository, life-related preaching We try to work our way consecutively through a book at a time, breaking the Bible into bite-sized chunks. Using the *Good News* Bible, we have tried to undo the lie that you need to be a 'book person' to understand the Scriptures. Our aim has been to create an enthusiasm for Scripture and so show that anyone can get something out of it. We want to see daily Bible reading as a part of everyone's life, especially for those with little formal education.

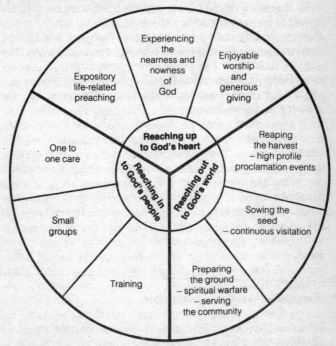

We also stress that Scripture is to be obeyed; it is not just a book full of the theory of religion. In it God is giving us, in the twentieth-century world, 'instruction for right living, so that the person who serves God may be fully qualified and equipped to do every kind of good deed' (2 Tim 3:16, 17). Being aware, however, that people do what you inspect, not what you expect, we follow up our Sunday preaching themes in our mid-week house groups. Here we can ensure that both understanding and application are taking place. Consecutive preaching also means we avoid preachers'

hobby-horses; we give the congregation a balanced diet, tackling sensitive subjects that might otherwise be avoided, eg divorce, homosexuality, racism and materialism. To assist this work of God's word in our lives, we have a small prayer team praying during the message.

Experiencing the nearness and nowness of God We are not content just to tell people of the things God used to do. He is not a 'has been' but an 'is now': is now 'bringing good news to the poor, liberty to captives, recovery of sight to the blind, and setting free the oppressed'. Consequently we pray for people during services, expecting God to work in their lives in some tangible way. Various outside ministries have aided our growth here, notably that of John Wimber's Vineyard teams. We appreciate all the gifts of the Holy Spirit and have open times of worship when all members of the body can participate. It is encouraging to hear local people talk about us as a church that truly does believe in God! Part of that reputation has been earned by praying for the sick in open-air services during the summer, or whenever we engage in open-air evangelism.

Enjoyable worship and generous giving It seems that biblical worship was rich, varied and above all enjoyable—with festivals, feasts, loud music, dancing, singing. We see celebration everywhere. Of all the people on earth, God's people have something worth getting excited about. So we have tried to make our public services full of opportunities for the congregation to express the joy of their new life in Christ. Music and singing are prominent, with a dedicated group of worship leaders and musicians up front. Time and again newcomers have been touched just by the sincerity and joy of the worship. We try to blend in some of the older hymns with the contemporary songs of today, as well as songs written by our own members.

This generous giving of praise to our great God is also anchored in the generous giving of our money. 'God loves a generous giver.' We stress that the true test of whether God has really touched our hearts is shown by what happens to our pockets. To teach generosity we began a few years ago to tithe our income as a church. God seemed to be pleased with this, and enabled us to increase the amount we gave away the following year. This has been the pattern every year since then. In a world that teaches and pressurises people to get all they can, we have sought to stand out from today's culture that falsely equates materialism with happiness. As we have tried to practise generosity, and to be 'a generous church in a selfish world', God has honoured us. It is indeed more blessed to give than to receive.

Reaching into God's people

Over the years a very loving and caring fellowship that embraces many cultures and that is very tolerant of many different backgrounds, has developed due to a strong emphasis on these principles:

One-to-one care People in the inner city need to feel they belong; life can be impersonal and lonely, even in the church. Little community spirit exists in Clapham Park—unlike nearby Brixton. To meet this need, we try to link everyone in the church into a 'care pair', with someone who will meet them at least monthly for prayer and mutual support. A new Christian would be linked with someone more established in the faith, who would take them through a 'basic beliefs' Bible study course. These care pairs ensure that many potential pastoral problems are anticipated and that newcomers quickly feel secure and a part of the fellowship.

Small groups In order to 'possess the land', we have sought to set up many different cell groups throughout the area. The smallest group is the 'Light in Every Street' group—a prayer group meeting to pray specifically for the block of flats or road where its members live. These prayer groups often contain Christians from other local churches and usually meet monthly. The next type of group is the fellowship group, each of our members being allocated to one of the many home-based groups covering the area. They meet fortnightly on a Thursday evening, each following a similar study outline based on the current theme of the Sunday teaching.

The leaders' task is to provide pastoral oversight of their members; they ensure that each person has a care pair and in some way contributes to the welfare of the group. Thus each group has someone responsible for worship, another for evangelism, for social activities (birthdays etc), refreshments, prayer requests, book reviews, missionary news, etc. These different representatives are gathered together periodically by the relevant church leaders (for example, worship leaders) to help train them or to pass on information for other group members, such as missionary news, or plans for evangelism.

The group leader meets regularly with the leadership team to chat and pray over any problems, and he or she also has access to the counselling team for referring any people with deep and persistent needs. There is also a termly breakfast for all fellowship group leaders, when I try to encourage them and show them where they fit in the overall strategy. We are hoping to increase the training element in leadership meetings next year.

A third type of small group is the common interest group, for example, Oasis—the group for young mothers to snatch a quiet hour's stimulating Bible study while the baby sleeps; or the Saturday evening fellowship group for those unable to attend a mid-week group; or the group of young Christian wives meeting to pray for the salvation of their husbands; or the Grapevine group for the singles (the divorced, bereaved, never married).

We love small groups and encourage our members to get together as often as possible and experience biblical 'koinonia'. As the number of groups has grown, so has our leadership base, and so has our confidence in open worship. Small groups have given many of our members a sense of identity and the thrill of being able to contribute something towards God's work. In an impersonal city, and a growing church, this sense of involvement and of belonging is an essential part of our quest to help build a healthy self-love in many who feel they count for little.

Training Having many opportunities for people to discover and exercise their gifts and talents, we also have to provide opportunities for training, if people are to develop to their fullest potential for the Lord. We do this on a central basis, drawing everyone from the area groups into training sessions, often led by full-time staff members. As I write we are running training sessions on counselling and on how to minister healing and deliverance. In the past we have covered personal evangelism, leading worship, and how to prepare and give a talk. We did tend to give training only when its need became apparent; in the future it would be good to develop a long-term balanced programme giving training the priority we say it should have.

Reaching out to God's world

Continuous evangelism has always characterised our church—it has to, otherwise we would die because of the rapid turnover of South London's population. This evangelism, however, has to meet the challenges of relating the gospel to several cultures. There is the local culture of native Londoners, which breaks down into two main groups: owner/occupiers and those living in rented accommodation. Then there is a large West Indian community, which again breaks itself down into those with a background sympathetic to religion, and a younger generation which has tended to reject Christianity as 'white man's' religion. The African community, mainly students, is also quite sizeable, as is the Muslim community. We have also been affected by the arrival of Yuppies, who have adopted parts of our area. Then there are the huge estates reflecting the alienation from society that many feel in the inner city, the symptoms of single-parent families (the highest number in the whole of Lambeth), juvenile crime, drug abuse, alcoholism, unemployment (especially among the black community).

The principles outlined below undergird our outreach, but the methods are continually being adapted as the Holy Spirit inspires creativity, and as we learn from our flops!

Preparing the ground The ground is hard and covered with many deep-rooted weeds. These we need to remove, and then we must dig the ground over before it can receive the seed. Going out on to the streets in praise marches has had a clear weed-killing effect. Our praises have not just been a strong (and attractive) public witness but have also been like a spiritual disinfectant, cleaning up and sweetening the spiritual climate. We now value praise marches as the foundation for our evangelism; our good works are the second. If praises kill the ground weeds, then our good deeds are the spade work that loosens the ground, softens people and gains us credibility in the community.

Both are essential if we are to get the community to listen to our message, for we are competing against so many others proclaiming messages at people (the politicians, police, National Front, social services, etc). We also need to stand out from among the cults and sects—the Mormons, Moonies and Jehovah's Witnesses are active on our streets. Good works, letting your light 'shine before people, so that they will see the good things you do and praise your Father in heaven' (Mt 5:16) have been a key to our not being dismissed as just another bunch of religious or political activists.

We have sought to serve the community according to the gifts of our members; hence, with over twenty gifted youth workers, our young people's and children's work is still seen by the public as our major form of Christian service. We still run Boys' Brigade and Girl Guides. However, because teenagers increasingly resist discipline and uniforms, we have broadened our youth work and now run three open youth clubs, led by a full-time Christian youth leader, Marc Bassot, who is funded by the Inner London Education Authority. Many families in the area have appreciated the support our youth leaders have given them in divorce, trouble with police and unemployment.

Similarly we have been able to develop a ministry to the over sixties in the area, as God was clearly giving us people gifted in working with older people. Our 'Caleb Club' now has contact with nearly 200 older folk, and access to a local home for a monthly service. We rejoice to see professions of faith as a result of this ministry. Catering for the other end of the age spectrum is Mosaic, a weekly mothers and toddlers club.

The most recent venture has been the opening of our family advice centre which we run with the help and expertise of two Christian social workers from Fegan's Homes as well as two of our own experienced counsellors. We open fortnightly for anyone to drop in for a chat, or for help and prayer. The value of this tangible expression of God's concern and love for the deprived is quite apparent, as are our two afternoon clubs for unemployed young people, run by our youth worker. We hope to extend this work by opening a morning Jobs Club under the auspices of the Manpower Services Commission.

Sowing Building on this background of praise and service, we regularly scatter the seeds of the gospel throughout the area, looking for signs of response. We have been privileged to have a full-time evangelist from the London City Mission, John Taylor, who spearheads our sowing programme, knocking on hundreds of doors each year, giving away free literature. We have held 'blitz nights' sending out fifty pairs to saturate an area. Teams from Operation Mobilisation, from Bible colleges, the Navigators and British Youth for Christ have also worked with us.

We give out invitations to the neighbourhood to various special events (Mothers' Day, Christmas, Easter, harvest) and try to link them with poster campaigns, matching posters in members' houses, shops, in the church centre and local tube stations. Our publicity team works hard to ensure a consistent image on all our literature, which appears (to judge by the return of our postage paid reply cards) to be well read and meeting needs. Over 100 people, for example, wrote back requesting more literature after the showing of the film *Jesus* at our local cinema. Helping to coordinate all this visiting and ensuring interested contacts receive follow-up visits is Paul Spiller, who works closely with John Taylor and spends mornings on administration and afternoons out visiting.

Reaping The final principle is this one: having dug the ground well and scattered the seed widely, a harvest will follow. Our job is to go out with the sickle and reap it. This we are tending to do more and more in the summer months, when we do what everyone else in Clapham and Brixton seems to do when the light nights and warm weather arrive—take to the streets! We enter the local midsummer festival on Clapham Common for the weeekend (closing church that Sunday), sell strawberries and cream and entertain the crowd with music and drama, interspersed with preaching and testimonies. In our counselling tent many come for prayer for healing and other needs, and we always see professions of faith. We have also taken our morning services in August outside into a nearby park. Before the services we marched round the adjacent estate singing and witnessing, inviting people to come to the service. At the end we always invite bystanders to 'have one on us'—a prayer by our members who move among the crowd looking for those God wants to meet with.

We run holiday clubs for children and we invite people to special guest services. We show gospel films; we put on evangelistic dinners. We invite groups to come and work with us for a mission (Navigators, Operation Mobilisation, Bible colleges etc). We were heavily involved in Luis Palau's Mission to London, both on Clapham Common in

1983 and at Queens Park Rangers' stadium in 1984. We saw many professions of faith from those missions as people in the community responded to our invitation to come with us and hear the evangelist.

Summer months are for getting out, out where the harvest is. Our joy is to report that the fields are indeed white and black and brown unto harvest!

The future

After surviving several threats to its life, Bonneville has grown into a medium-sized church. We now face the challenges of breaking through the barriers that inhibit medium-sized churches growing into large churches. We are looking at our leadership structure and are now in the process of changing over from the traditional Baptist structure of minister-deacons-members to that of team leadership. This sharing of pastoral responsibility with three other elders (one of them, Dave Austin, is also full-time and is undertaking theological training at Spurgeons College) has meant a lot to me, releasing me and giving me a new lease of life and fresh zeal to use my own spiritual gifts as effectively as possible for the future growth of our church.

Shared leadership also enables us to face necessary change more bravely than when one is leading alone! We sense changes need to be made in our youth work and also in our overall weekly timetable as we place more emphasis on training. Our Sundays tend to be the very opposite of a 'day of rest' and also need to be changed. Our prayer life continually battles against spiritual inertia—the early morning prayer meetings and half nights of prayer are not the power-houses they should be.

Challenges still lie in front of us, but we are in good heart. Our name 'Bonneville' means 'a good place'. That is what we intend to make it.

A good place for Jesus. A launching pad where our

victorious Lord can reach out into a hurting multi-racial community with his healing, saving touch. A place where the lost sheep, now found, can be brought back, nurtured, fed and trained then to go back out and 'make disciples also' in Jesus' powerful name. We will not be content until our church makes Satan tremble.

Chapter 4

The Parish of Bestwood
Nottingham

Mavis Bexon

The parish of Bestwood in Nottingham used to consist of three churches serving three estates: Bestwood, Bestwood Park and Top Valley. Mavis Bexon, then deaconess of the parish, writes of the years of her ministry there. As in the case of Skelmersdale (Chapter 1), the people of Bestwood were often lonely and desperate. However, members of these three churches came together and with the support of St John's College in Nottingham worked and prayed in the community for social services, counselling and reconciliation. Out of the heartaches came a measure of healing for Bestwood.

The Revd Mavis Bexon has worked for twenty-four years in the Anglican ministry, mostly in urban areas. She talks openly as we meet her in this chapter of both the 'successes' and 'failures' she and her fellow-ministers—among them Eddie Neale—encountered in Nottingham.

Now serving in Derby, Mavis is on a new estate, gathering people together to form a church. There is no building, so all the activities go on in her home, where forty to fifty people meet to worship each Sunday. Having spent such a big part of her life living in flats she is now enjoying a house and garden, which have turned her into something of a home-maker. She also enjoys reading, walking and going to concerts.

The three estates

Some time between the two world wars slum clearance programmes began in Nottingham. One of the results of this was the creation of the Bestwood council estate. Bestwood was built where sheep had once grazed the hills. To enter any of the solid red-brick houses it is necessary to go down a steep flight of steps from the pavement. The combination of the slopes and small windows makes the houses dark inside.

The roads are designed to form circles. Imagine dropping a pebble into a pond and the circles rippling outwards. Here you more or less have, though on a larger scale, an aerial view of the estate. But this arrangement gives no friendly grouping of dwellings—just long roads whose house numbers go into the hundreds.

The school had originally been in an encampment of large huts. Baptist church members from a more salubrious part of Nottingham were allowed to use these as a base when they pioneered children's work and started a Sunday school for the hundreds of children around.

Eventually, in the 1950s, a church building went up—a long, thin, tall structure which from a distance is usually mistaken for a fire station. In the same grounds is an older hall which had originally been used for worship but then, more recently, was little used.

Fifteen years or so after the Bestwood estate was completed, an adjacent area was built on by the council, and

thus the Bestwood Park estate was born. This estate benefited from the mistakes made in Bestwood: shorter roads
linked the grouping of houses, with green patches left and
mature trees not cut down indiscriminately. In fact some of
the houses were bordered by parts of the large, rambling
wood.

Legend has it that Charles I gave Nell Gwyn as much land
in this area as she could ride around on horseback. With her
interest in hunting, she had deliberately ridden round the
best part of the woods, hence the name Bestwood.
Bestwood Park had all the facilities Bestwood lacked: a
shopping precinct with full-time post office, a rent office,
police station, clinic and doctor's surgery. There were
schools, and no fewer than four churches sprang up. The
Methodist, Pentecostal and Roman Catholic churches all
had good buildings. The Methodist was in a prime spot on
a main road, near the shopping precinct, but the Church of
England had only a Portakabin in an out-of-the-way
location.

When I visited the area, Ron Clarke, who was then vicar,
showed me around these two estates in his parish. Then he
stopped on the top of a hill, and his hand swept over the
massive area in front and to the side of us. 'As far as you can
see and farther,' he said, 'is going to be built on. It will be
a third estate in the parish called "Top Valley".'

And so Christian work began on this third estate. Deaconess Pam Harvey (now a deacon) was working with Ron
Clarke at the time. She managed to get one of the first flats
to be built on Top Valley. As a new house or flat became
occupied, she would visit. A group of people soon grew
together. As schools went up, Pam was one of the first to
visit headteachers. She was the contact for social workers;
she was a founder member of the community council, and
she started a social workers' lunch club.

Eventually she gathered enough people together to have
a service of worship. First they met in a house the council let
them use, temporarily, as a community house. A year later

the diocese built a dual-purpose place of worship: a long, brick building with kitchen, hall, loos and a very small store place. This has served successfully to house Guides, Brownies, Cubs and Scouts, Red Cross and the local worshipping community with all its associated meetings.

A matter of months after this building went up Ron moved on and Pam was left looking after three churches and a parish of 35,000 people. When the Revd Eddie Neale was appointed vicar at the end of 1976, Pam was also ready to move on, and so it came about that I replaced her in the early part of 1977, living in the flat that had been her home and working in the parish of Bestwood with special responsibility for Top Valley.

Eddie had been there long enough to be able to look at the whole of the work in a fairly detached way. There were many social problems. Bestwood had a high rate of crime. Top Valley seemed to specialise in unhappy, depressed people, and a lot of my work was liaison with the psychiatric social worker. People had been moved from areas where they had lived all their lives. They had been near to shops and pubs and a great deal of activity. Top Valley was five miles from the town and there was tremendous loneliness— in many cases despair.

With less than 1 per cent of the inhabitants confessing any church allegiance at all, Eddie and I asked each other how we were going to be most effective in bringing the good news of Jesus to these people. The most obvious thing to do seemed to be to ask the members of the church. They were the ones from whom everything should spring.

And so a day conference took place in the summer of 1977. We went to an old house, then occupied by the army, who gave us the use of various facilities and the grounds which were extensive and quite beautiful. It was just out-side the parish, so neutral ground for all three churches. The Revd Ian Saville, the bishop's adviser on mission, led our thoughts, and the result of the day was that we formed a three-year plan. Details had to be worked out by the group appointed for the purpose, but we had fixed on the target of doubling the size of our congregations by the end of the three years. There was a great deal of discussion about this. Were we going for quantity or quality? In other words, did we want to fill pews or did we want to build a church—a group of committed Christians?

We decided that, in an area like ours, only the second suggestion was possible. It was right against local custom to be connected with the church in any way. The possibility of nominal membership was remote.

The three-year plan

First year—looking at ourselves

The three-year plan was put into operation. The first year involved looking at ourselves, thinking what we were doing and asking ourselves why we were doing it. We thought it was good to get the three different groupings together, so we had a parish social committee and arranged one event each month. A weekly mid-week fellowship took turns in meeting in the three different churches. We felt we wanted to worship together as a parish on a regular basis. Because the geographical distances made this impossible on a Sunday, we decided that once a month the mid-week fellowship should be a service of Holy Communion.

The ministry of healing had already been discussed. In fact one service of healing had taken place before my arrival, instigated by a member of the Bestwood Park church who was suffering from multiple sclerosis. Eddie had done a series of Bible studies on the ministry of healing, and we began to read together a book that was very popular at the time—*Healing*, by Francis MacNutt. The custom evolved of giving an opportunity for the ministry of healing in the monthly joint Communion service. This was not advertised but was for our own fellowships as a normal part of church life. There was a great air of expectancy around, a contagious enthusiasm and an awareness that God was at work. 'Expectancy' is the right word to use for one of our first experiences of healing.

One couple from Bestwood who had been married for some time desperately wanted a child but did not see any hope of pregnancy. The years were passing by, and they were praying as earnestly as Hannah had done in the Temple (1 Sam 1) all those centuries before. Soon there was as much rejoicing in Bestwood as there had been in Israel when a pregnancy was confirmed. The prospective parents were always quite sure their barrenness had been healed at that first healing service when others had prayed for them with such fervour.

A woman from Bestwood Park testified to another kind of healing. Her husband had left her and subsequently divorced and remarried. She had done everything possible to keep the marriage together, even living with him for two years when she knew he was having an affair with somebody else. After he had left she still hoped he would come back. Even after the divorce she believed they would get together again. Then one day he gave her the date of his second marriage. Still she prayed it would be prevented. But it happened. And the healing that eventually came to her was not only the healing of the bitterness she felt towards both her husband and his new wife, but also the feeling of failure and the low estimation of her own value. The greatest sign of the depth of this healing was when the new wife was ill and the first wife visited her in hospital and ministered to her.

The first healing we knew at the Top Valley church was actually independent of the healing service in our own parish. As part of our 'sorting-out' year we attended a festival of praise at a Nottingham church. At some point we were asked to link hands and pray for each other. As we did this an elderly member of our group felt a rush of warmth going down her side. When we came out she was skipping up and down the road, for she had not bent her knees in years and was showing us she had been healed from arthritis. It was a case of receiving what she had not asked for.

On another occasion somebody was brought round to my flat by one of our Top Valley Christians. This woman was riddled with guilt and ready to accept forgiveness. Perhaps the person who had brought her could have prayed with her, but she wanted the support of someone else; and so we prayed with and for her. As we did so, we laid hands on her to assure her of her forgiveness. It was not until a few days later that we discovered she had been healed of a malignant tumour at the same time. As her sins were pronounced forgiven, the tumour on her knee had dissolved. And when she went to the specialist the next day, as arranged, he looked in bewilderment at her charts and could find no answer for the healing.

Sadly she did not stay in the church for very long. The pressure of old friends and old habits was too attractive to her and, as far as I know, she now has nothing to do with any church. What this teaches us is that God out of his generosity sometimes chooses to do things we humans would never be kind enough to do. Thus, as we reached the end of the first year, the churches were being strengthened in their faith; they were seeing exciting things happening as they entered the second phase of their plan.

Second year—a year of renewal and the sorting out of structures

The year started with a week of meetings on renewal. I suppose the greatest result was when people saw fresh possibilities in their own lives. Many of our people were used to being dismissed every time they spoke, and their confidence had gone. But now there was a new realisation of who they were (people made by God and belonging to him) and of the potential they had through the power of the Holy Spirit.

Together we looked at the fruits of the Spirit (Gal 5:22) and saw what we were capable of becoming. The inclusion of self-control in the list of the fruits was new to many. One of the Top Valley people told me she knew there must be something in this Christianity business because when her neighbour 'caught it', she stopped throwing saucepans at her husband and things were much quieter! Others found they could exercise greater patience towards their children. Most of all, love filled us. In this way people were attracted to the church. They saw God through the love shown in Christians (1 Jn 4:12).

As we discovered the fruits of the Spirit we also discovered the gifts. If the fruits showed us what we could become, the gifts showed us what we could do. We took a weekend away, borrowing a teachers' training college in Derbyshire for the occasion. The Revd David Gillett, who was then on the staff of St John's College, Nottingham, led the weekend. One of the things he did with us was to help us discover what gifts other people had. We sat in a circle, and each person within it had to write down the gifts he felt each other person in the group had. This prevented a false modesty on the one hand and pride on the other.

As time went by and we tried to discover how people's gifts could be used, it became clear that some structures had to change. Until now the parish church in Bestwood had seen the other two churches very much as its children, but if the children were to grow and reach maturity, they had to have the space to do it.

The main parish church was the only one with wardens. Although each church had its local committee, the only legal council was the parochial one, which was heavily weighted by members of the parish church. Hence we worked out a new scheme with the archdeacon by which each church had equal representation from the three churches. The council would now be composed of the minister from each church, the two wardens, the deanery synod representative, the treasurer and two elected members—making a council of twenty-one people.

To make space for new people to use their gifts and so develop their potential, we passed a resolution that nobody should hold church office (wardens, treasurers and secretaries) for longer than three years. We later changed this to five because it seemed to take that long for people to get to grips with a job, and the church benefited from their experience, though we retained the rule that no one should be on the council longer than three consecutive years. This prevented one person remaining warden or treasurer for forty years, as happens in many churches. It was a painful exercise for the parish church, for with privilege came responsibility. Until this point any money had gone to the parish treasurer, who had paid the bills, but from now on each church would be responsible for its own finances and each would contribute to a central fund for the diocesan quota and for such staff expenses as were allowed.

Although young and small, the Top Valley church readily agreed to the plan. Bestwood Park was less eager partly because they were at first without a minister of their own. The Revd Ted Lyons was to join us later that year; and with their own minister at the helm, they soon grew in confidence and laughed at their initial hesitation.

It became obvious during this year that if we were going to welcome newcomers into the worshipping community, the services had to be adapted to accommodate them. We were out to reach people to whom church services were alien. We needed to be able not only to communicate with them, but also to make the services a time when they could freely worship with meaning and understanding.

Bestwood had attracted committed Christians to a 9 am Communion service, which Ron Clarke had made the main teaching point of the day. There were also services at

10.15 am and 6.30 pm. Because we were trying to accommodate those who were not used to attending church it became important to give more attention to the 10.15 am family service. Many local people were given the opportunity to take part in this service, and it became lively, warmhearted and welcoming. Later on, Communion became part of the family service on a monthly basis.

Bestwood Park, which had been without a full-time minister for some years, had its only service at 6.30 pm. This was well attended and had good, lively singing. Sunday school was held in the morning. Eventually Bestwood Park united with the Methodist church. Whereas Bestwood Park had only a temporary building, the Methodists had a good building in a prime position on the main road near the shopping centre. In the late 1970s the Bestwood Park church had been approached about uniting with the Methodists. Twice the Anglicans had rejected the proposal, but when the question was brought up a third time, Bestwood Park was more confident. Anxiety about their lost identity was appeased as Ted Lyons took over and everyone was caught up with the enthusiasm of the three-year plan. Sadly, some were totally against this and eventually left the church; some joined other congregations, but others dropped away altogether. Meanwhile, Bestwood Park was now able to have a family service with children going out for Sunday school at the appropriate time. The evenings became times of informality, more often than not following a Methodist order of service rather than a set liturgy.

Top Valley was too new to have had much of a pattern. The church had tried many different ideas and was still working towards what was appropriate. Without a regular Communion service, members had been expected to go over to Bestwood, a twenty-minute walk over the playing fields. To add to their problems, their building was very restrictive. The only rooms suitable for Sunday school were the kitchen and a tiny vestry, from which everything could be heard in the main room. They tried holding Sunday school immediately after church, but that meant the teachers were not free to talk to people at the end of the service. It also meant children of Christian parents sat through two hours of teaching. (I cannot remember where I picked up the quotation of H L Moden, who says Sunday school is 'a prison in which children do penance for the evil conscience of their parents'—but I can believe it when Sunday school is separated from the main worshipping body.) There was a general feeling that families should worship together, that there was little place for the unaccompanied child. We remember the great campaign of some years ago with the slogan 'Don't send a child to Sunday school. Take him.' Still, after a while, we had to ask ourselves some serious questions about the rights of children. In an area like ours it was a very big step for an adult to walk over the threshold of a church. Did that mean children must miss out? I could not help thinking of some of the great people in church history who had become Christians in their childhood in spite of, rather than because of, their parents. So, yes, there was a place for the unaccompanied child, and that child had to be a part of the family of the church.

Eventually the local authority built a community centre near the church in Top Valley, and we rented it for half an hour each Sunday morning. The children were able to begin and end in the body of the church but go out for their own teaching during the sermon.

Having had two years to organise ourselves and our churches and—by sheer enthusiasm—to reach our neighbours, we felt we were ready for stage three.

Third year—a year of evangelism

Again we went away for the weekend at the start of this year. It was snowing at the time and sledging made a good activity for the 'free' periods. There was a good feeling of being united for the task ahead. We had the help of St John's College, Nottingham. Thirty students were involved, ten being assigned to each church. David Gillett, the tutor who was in charge from the college side, gave most of the talks.

We continued to have monthly social events with a view to drawing outsiders in. There were evangelistic house groups led by the students. All those involved in the churches were geared up to spreading the good news of Jesus.

We ran a community newspaper which was delivered to the 12,000 houses in the parish every month. The parish magazine also went out each month; it aimed both to inform the congregations of what was going on within the churches but also to give some teaching on issues facing the church: remarriage of divorcees in church, ordination of women and urban priority problems. Many such issues have since been aired or decided on a national level, and we would hope that the people in the local churches helped to influence the decisions and understand them once they are made.

The purpose of the community paper was outreach. One of its aims was to foster some identity as a community. Another was to point out the good things that were happening, to raise people's expectations and to lift them out of lethargy and sometimes despair. We called it *Best News*. The logo we designed made a play on the word 'best' in Bestwood and Bestwood Park, so the title became 'Best News for Bestwood, Bestwood Park and Top Valley'. On the front page there was always a testimony, accompanied by a photograph. We took our own photographs, and though many were taken with cheap automatics, they came out very well. It was a brave act for people to have their photograph and testimony there for their neighbours to see; it meant they had a great deal to live up to. Understandably, some refused because of this.

The large task of distributing the papers needed careful

organising, and the distributors were—like those in photographs—'marked' men and women. Generally people distributed in the area in which they lived. This took courage, but it also presented good opportunities.

Inside were reports of positive things happening in the community; neighbourhood watch, street parties etc. It meant we were constantly in touch with all the institutions in the community for news and photographs. We covered school events and sheltered housing. So, apart from the general usefulness of this service, the teachers and local people were ready to co-operate with us as we came to the end of the three-year plan. A week of concentrated evangelism rounded off the three years and heralded some other new beginnings.

Week of evangelism

There is nothing so exciting as a large group of people out to achieve a common purpose. The local Christians were fully involved, as were the thirty students from St John's College and David Gillett. Church families accommodated the students in their respective areas. Each day the entire team met for lunch. This was the time we planned, prayed and shared. Each church organised events suitable to its particular area.

Top Valley has a comprehensive school of 1,300 pupils. With no hall big enough to hold the entire school at one time, each year held an assembly on a different day of the week, starting with the first-year children on Mondays. The headmaster allowed us to lead these assemblies each day. The junior schools were more cautious, but once a guitarist had been allowed to teach them a song, barriers came down and we had an invitation to come back.

We also went into sheltered housing complexes, community centre and playgroup. Evangelistic house groups were going on all the week. For everybody there was a barn dance with a break in the middle when David Gillett taught a song and spoke about Jesus. As the youth organisations met in the church during the week, we went along and invited parents. On the Saturday we rented the local swimming baths for a fun day, which attracted many dads. We had a ploughman's supper afterwards in the church and a further opportunity for direct evangelism.

Sunday was harvest festival. A student spoke at the morning service and David Gillett in the evening. Throughout the parish many stayed behind for counselling after the Sunday services, and quite a few made commitments. These were not casual people come in out of the blue, but were those we had known, nurtured and particularly prayed for—often husbands of Christian wives or parents of Christian children.

Many of the people we knew well had had unhappy childhoods or some kind of disturbed background. Very often they were overloaded with guilt. It is my opinion that the blood-and-thunder preacher, determined to convince people of their sins, has no place in a parish like ours. People were only too aware of their sins. Their problem was this: could they be forgiven?

Another problem was the difficulty of establishing trust. If everybody you have ever trusted has let you down, how can you trust Christians who are trying to help you? But, more important, how can you trust God? I spent quite a lot of time trying to help one person. As a young man he had discovered, by accident, that the person he thought was his mother was really his grandmother and the young woman he thought was his 'sister' had actually given birth to him. The experience so affected him that he ran away from home and for a very long time he would have nothing to do with his family. But it also meant he had a built-in distrust of everyone and everything. He said he experienced agony from the moment he left for work in the morning until he arrived home in the evening. He imagined that as soon as he was out of the house his wife would either leave him or take in another man. His day was punctuated by the times he could get to a phone and check up.

This man received no relief from his obsession. He refused medical help and, although there were times when he wanted to be healed, the times when he wanted to remain as he was were more frequent. We often wonder why God heals some people and not others. There is no answer. God is God and does what he thinks best.

There was a great deal of supportive work to do with those who became Christians. Some experienced liberty as the 'burden of guilt rolled away'. Others took some time to experience absolute forgiveness, like the old lady who would say, 'But I've been such a wicked woman.' We would go through the gospel again and assure her of forgiveness. She would be assured, temporarily, but a few days later would return to say, 'But I've been such a wicked woman'. Happily, she died quite peacefully in one of the periods when she was enjoying the experience of forgiveness.

Social concern

As Eddie Neale's reputation for involvement with the 'down and outs' increased he became overloaded in Bestwood with people who needed help, and launched many schemes to help them, filling the under-used church halls at St Matthew's with activity. An advice centre was set up which employed many, with a barrister volunteering to give free legal advice. Many job opportunity schemes were set up, and a resource centre for the area was provided. The centre began to produce its own newsletter, and the work grew.

Later, Ted Lyons initiated another advice centre at Bestwood Park. Since joining with the Methodists they too had spacious accommodation and could become involved with all sorts of social concern.

Top Valley's small building housed very successful

Guides and Brownies, Scouts and Cubs and St John Ambulance, but for further activities it decided to throw in its lot with the community centre.

As I already mentioned, Pam Harvey had started the social workers' lunch club in Top Valley, and I joined when I started to work there. By then the work was flourishing. The house next to her flat (later mine) was a temporary community centre called the 'community house'. In this were held youth clubs, playgroup and pensioners' lunch club. Members of the church were involved in all of these. When the council wanted the house back for a family dwelling, the community council was offered a prefabricated bungalow as a permanent facility.

Then Keith, a church member, dreamed up another idea. There was one old building in Top Valley, now vacated and about to be pulled down. Attached to it was a 100-yard extension that had been used as offices. Keith worked out that this extension could be lifted up and put on the site earmarked for community purposes. He arranged to see the leisure services' director about it and asked me if I would go to support him. This I gladly did and was truly amazed to sit and listen to the plan he had worked out with careful consideration for technical detail.

The leisure services' director said to me, 'Your predecessor agreed to the bungalow.'

'She wouldn't have done so had there been the possibility of something bigger,' I told him.

So it happened as Keith had suggested. A lot of local work was involved and months of agonising meetings and disagreement among local groups finally resulted in a good centre with a hall big enough for youth work and the inevitable discos, as well as the employment of a full-time warden and office staff. The playgroups and pensioners' lunch clubs now take place there, and a care group which was started by the church was transferred to the centre.

Christians throughout the parish were involved in community activity; we were taking Jesus to the world. Mothers were voluntary helpers or dinner ladies in the schools. They helped in nurseries and ran playgroups. They organised lunch clubs or just did the washing-up. Others met people in the pub or over their fences and washing-lines.

The original aim of doubling our congregations was more than fulfilled, but there followed years of steady working in the church and community. There were many rewards but also many disappointments; this is so in all Christian work because people cannot be put into boxes, labelled and have the lid shut on them, then put on the shelves all neatly classified.

Nevertheless, the people we have seen grow into Christian maturity have been a tremendous encouragement. During the interregnum after Eddie left, Bestwood was led very ably and flourished under the ministry of local people. Ted has also left Bestwood Park, but the marks of his ministry remain. As for Top Valley, I have just conducted the wedding service for a couple who waited for me to be ordained before they married. They each came into church contact when their lives had been shattered. They are now restored, healed and together, taking a very responsible part in the life of the church and community. What greater reward could there be?

Three more churches have been added to the parish, and I guess the new staff will get the congregations together. I am sure they are looking into the future, asking the important question of each other, 'Which way do we go next?'

Chapter 5

St Peter's Church, Cardiff

Fr Philip Scanlan

Father Philip Scanlan was born and brought up in the busy parish of St Peter's. As he himself says, his common background with the parishioners has helped him deeply both in his pastoral care and in his relationships in the community as a whole. With four fellow-priests—all full-time— he celebrates three daily Masses and five Sunday Masses. This coming together for the breaking of bread is the centre and source of the church's life and ministry. Here the parish re-enters the covenant initiated by Christ's death and resurrection, and receives the strength to go out and live the gospel in the city beyond.

The parish around St Peter's is heavily built up, typical of many areas in Cardiff. It has grown since the nineteenth century from a close-knit community of terraced housing, through severe industrial decline, to a new world of housing estates, some tourism, and commerce. The city is changing so fast that the pace of change amazes even a long-time resident such as Fr Scanlan.

St Peter's is a large parish of just over 4,000 Catholics. It has grown in 125 years from a small cluster of houses near the cathedral-like church to a sprawling network of streets which spreads out from the centre of the city to the now-distant boundaries. It is a parish which grew out of the needs of the teeming thousands who sought work in the Industrial Revolution and its aftermath.

Like any parish, St Peter's is a community—it is people; and as such, it has all the inbuilt richness of human nature, the never exhausted variety of God's creation. It is a People of saints and sinners—and many in between; it is a community of profound human growth and of the lowest reaches of human wretchedness. In this people, in the parish community, God's message of salvation has to be preached and lived. Here, as in any human community, we find sanctity alongside indifference and rejection—and, between these two extremes, so many who struggle to 'do their best'.

It is in the ministry of the confessional that the Priest is brought face to face with the effects of sin and evil in ordinary lives. Here, the one who is close to God recognises by that very closeness that there is still need for healing and reconciliation. Sometimes after a life of sin and almost complete rejection of God, a person is led back and there is the immense joy of sharing in the return of a lost sheep. But it is the day-to-day struggles to be faithful and to overcome human weakness which make up the larger part of this ministry. I can remember more than one occasion when one who had been weighed down by sin for many years came to receive this healing touch and to give thanks to God.

Change

In this parish there has been great change, a change which reflects that of a broader community of the city. Once an industrial centre of world renown, Cardiff has had to adjust to the decline of her industry and find a new life built upon commerce, tourism and the arts. As one who was born and brought up in this city, I am still amazed at the speed of change—the building of new roads, estates, shops, hospitals.... And yet, there is still a constancy about it all, and that constancy derives from the people who make the city and the parish.

The changes that have taken place coincided to an extent with the break up of the very close-knit communities of the turn of the century, communities formed very often on the common bond of a Catholic life and faith. They were communities largely made up of long rows of terraced houses—houses where the front door was always open and everybody seemed to know everybody else's business. But they were communities, too, in which the sorrows and the joys of one were shared by all. In time, these communities, of which St Peter's parish was an early example, had to yield before rehousing schemes, the closing of large industrial complexes, and a new restlessness in society that undermined the stability and much of the security of former times.

These changes were probably far more profound than any of us realised at the time; change in the local community only reflected more radical changes in the world at large, especially following World War II. Of course, this changing world could not and did not leave the Church untouched. Inspired by the Council of Pope John XXIII, the Church has responded to the challenge always implicit in change. The parish, too, has been forced to change; sometimes painfully, sometimes reluctantly and always slowly, new attitudes, new insights and a new vision have taken root. The community that is now St Peter's parish is one in which practice, attitudes, priorities have been fashioned both by the society in which we live, but also by the inspirations of the vision of the Church arising out of the Vatican Council. Moving about the parish day by day, one sees these changes revealed in so many different ways and situations.

In former times, the Priest 'held the reins' and controlled all decision-making and most of the activities within the parish. Partly due to the shortage of Priests, but mainly to one of the most important and far-reaching reforms of modern times, parishioners are now being urged to take on more of the active responsibility for their church and their parish. It is now the members of the parish who manage the parish hall, its finance and maintenance; the people arrange functions and exercise an active apostolate to the poor, the housebound and the sick. Although always responsible to the Priest, these groups and individuals are changing the parish from one which in every aspect of its life depended upon the Priest, to one which lives by its own energy and insight and vision. The Priest, meanwhile, released from many administrative duties, can give himself more to the essentially spiritual ministry for which he was ordained.

One hears stories told by the older generation of how, in pre-war days, the Priest had such authority and prestige that he was often called upon to act in the role of police-man-cum-arbitrator in domestic quarrels, in stopping street fights or in keeping youngsters out of bad ways. That kind of authority and prestige has largely disappeared; the Priest is now seen more as a leader who serves the community, not from a position of power, but in charity. Although we might look back with some criticism on the way things were in those far-off days, we need to remember the times and the society. On balance, one can be thankful that we have returned more to the image of the Priest in the role of shepherd, one who shares with his people all the human frailties and who, though not having all the answers, like them and with them, is reaching out for the ideal which is holiness.

The People of God

By its history and growth, the parish has a large number of elderly or housebound, many of whom have lived in the parish and even in their homes, all their lives. In years gone by—sometimes strangely called the 'good old days'—these people often suffered great hardship: real poverty, sickness and disease, appalling housing conditions and the effects of war all brought 'hard times'. And yet one so often comes across an unflinching faith that can still say with utter sincerity: 'God is good; he always looks after me.'

Tom was a man who had been a merchant seaman before working for many years in the Cardiff docks. He had raised a large family through hard times and was overjoyed when one of his sons became a Priest. Then, suddenly, at the age of forty, his son died of a heart attack. When I went to visit the home, there were many people already there—relatives, family, friends—and above the conversation I heard a voice say in some distress: 'Why? He was so young and could have done so much good.' Tom looked up and said firmly: 'You must never question—it's God's will and God is good...' and Tom meant every word. Tom and his wife are still alive, though frail and weak now in old age, and I know that their lives have never been the same since that day when their son died. But I also know that, in spite of the deep and lasting pain, they have never lost faith in the God who took their son to himself.

The pains and sufferings of life lead some people closer to God; but the pain is too great for others, and God is rejected in moments of deep anguish. In the two large hospitals within the parish, we so often have to face the agonies of physical pain and death itself; there, the pain of bereavement requires the healing balm of prayer and the sacraments of the Church. Perhaps the most painful of all such experiences is to share in the death of a baby. The great joy and pride of the parents in their child gives way to deep anxiety and then to the awful pain and resentment when the baby dies. One night I received an urgent call to the children's ward at the Royal Infirmary where a child of seven months was clearly near to death after a lengthy illness. The distraught parents had already lost their first child at the age of six months and were now faced with the same tragedy once again. But through all their tears there was no bitterness—only a deep sadness and longing. They decided to take the child home to Malaysia for burial, and before they left I celebrated Mass in their flat. In that mysterious way of grace, they derived strength and courage in those moments of prayer and Communion. Later on, when they returned to continue their studies at the university, they were given the gift of a third child, who is now two years old. Every time I see him, I recall that night in the hospital when his little sister died, and I give thanks not only that he has survived, but also for the faith and love of his parents which were such an example and inspiration for me.

For in these moments, it is the Priest, too, who needs to be open to the Spirit of God in order that the pastoral need of the suffering People of God may find support and strength.

In this parish, as in all others, there are those who, for a variety of reasons, have drifted away from the full life of the church. Christ, the Good Shepherd, is always searching for the lost sheep and for those who wander in dangerous ways; and he does this in and through the community of his Church. In practice, contact with the Church is maintained by the delivery to homes of newsletters, information sheets and copies of the parish magazine—so the door is never finally shut.

Annie was an elderly lady who, when her frail health permitted, made a special effort to be at Mass each Sunday. But as time passed, this became impossible, and I used to take Holy Communion to her at home every week. Annie grew weaker, and her family took it in turns to look after her and to be with her, rather than let her go into hospital. During my visits I came to know some of her family and grandchildren. One day, her daughter asked me to return later on to have a chat with her. This I did, and during our conversation, she poured out a long and complicated history of why and how she had abandoned the Church and built for herself a life in which there was no place for God or the Church. And yet, constantly at the back of her mind, there was an unrest, a feeling of loss.

As she spent more time with her mother, she was brought once again into contact with the Church, but this was not the Church she had rejected—here she found a caring warmth which she could identify as that of the caring Christ. At the end of her story I asked her if she felt that she wanted to take up again the full life of the Church, to find peace and reconciliation. When she asked how and when this could be, I said 'Now.' There and then, she received the healing touch of Christ and the restoration to that close friendship with him which he prayed for. She never looked back and when, a week later, her mother died, she faced her loss with a new-found strength and serenity.

Prayer

In so many, we discover a really profound prayer life— sometimes based on traditional forms of prayer, but also now embracing new forms. Prayer groups have been established and have encouraged many to learn to pray spontaneously for the first time; the riches of Scripture have been opened to many in this way and the prayer-form of Taizé has found a response in young and old alike, providing as it does a silence and calm which together satisfy a deep need.

Our ministry

As in society, so in the Church and in the parish, an awareness of others and of our common responsibility and duty
towards one another has found expression in societies
formed to minister to the needs of the poor and needy. But
in individuals, too, the awareness has led to commitment
and self-giving in areas relating to the defence of innocent
life, justice and peace, housing problems, care for the socially deprived and the mentally and physically handicapped. This vision of the common brotherhood of man, arising out of Christ's fundamental principle 'As you did it to
one of these, you did it to me' has stirred a consciousness in
the parish. Hence the Church has created a very thriving
and active Third World group, the function of which is not
only to raise funds, but also to foster among the parishioners an attitude of mind and heart which embraces the
spiritual and material needs of Christ's poor.

During the past four years, the group has raised over
£10,000 to send two Land Rovers to the missions in Tan-
zania, and another £10,000 has been raised to buy a tractor
for another part of the same country. As a constant service
to the missions, containers are sent out twice a year with
virtually everything one can think of, including—on one
occasion—a kitchen sink! I have seen ladders, a bicycle, a
cement-mixer, box upon box of clothes, medical supplies,
shoes, school text-books, all stored away for collection en
route to Africa. Each year a specific project is chosen in
partnership with other parishes in Cardiff to be sponsored
by the Lenten fasting and almsgiving voluntarily undertaken in preparation for the celebration of Easter.
Ethiopia, Kenya, Vietnam, India and Peru have all
benefited from these projects, and they have given the community a deeper appreciation of the reality of hunger and
homelessness.

Cardiff is a university city and 'bed-sit land' for many students lies within the parish. Though it is sometimes difficult for students to become fully integrated, yet it is a joy and inspiration to see so many young adults here sharing in our parish worship each Sunday. Overseas students—who are often away from home for two or three years—rightly look to the parish community for support and warmth in times of loneliness and homesickness. Some of these students have found ways of practical involvement in the life of the parish, either in the various societies or in the countless fetching and carrying tasks which are so necessary in a large parish. One has offered his services as a driver of the parish minibus, which makes two trips each Sunday to bring the elderly to Mass; another has been prepared as a catechist in the parish; yet another has set up a small workshop in the cellar of the presbytery where she can practise her art of ceramic design. Others have become involved in the over-eighteens group. In small ways, some of the students living in the parish have begun to find a place in the life of the community.

Though the unity of the parish community is derived essentially from the celebration of the Mass, it is also built up in the more human social contacts by which people come to know their neighbour much more deeply.

As a regular part of parish life, social functions are arranged sometimes just to get people together, but also sometimes for a specific charity: an oxygen monitor was presented to the children's ward at the Royal Infirmary, and half the cost of an orthopedic bed has been raised in this way. In these social gatherings, in the preparation and performance of the annual pantomime, and in being able to share company in pleasant surroundings, the unity of faith and charity, which is the sign of Christ's presence, is deepened and bears much fruit.

We are fortunate in that, over the years, much effort has been made to provide the facilities in which these social meetings can take place. A large hall was built in 1954, and I can remember as a very young parishioner how the collecting of funds to pay for the hall seemed to go on and on—everything seemed to be for the 'parish hall fund'. Now, as parish Priest, I can understand the struggle involved in raising the money needed to build the hall. More recently, a property already owned by the parish has been renovated and modernised for use as a parish centre where societies and individuals can meet, not only socially but also for meetings and spiritual events. All of these facilities are means by which to build up an identity in faith and charity among the people of the parish.

Pilgrims together

In this parish, we are travelling together, but along personal and unique paths. Each one, according to his or her vocation and circumstances, has been called to live the life of the gospel. Together, Priest and People form this pilgrim Church which journeys through time to its eternal destination with God. The parish community, like the individuals which make it up, has to struggle to overcome human frailty and weakness in order to reveal Christ to our world. On this journey, the Priest has to try to lead, to provide all that is necessary for the community to achieve its purpose.

This means not only to officiate at the celebration of Mass or the sacraments, but also to animate the vitality and energy of God's People in living the gospel message. It is often just to give encouragement and reassurance, to show interest, and to 'be around'. It means setting up structures within the parish which enable the community to live its life even if the Priest is away or sick. Here again, the Priest will need to lead the way because many will have been brought up in a church and in a parish where 'Father' did everything. Consultation and a sharing of decision-making are part of the process of making the community more self-reliant than in the past. For myself, this has meant trying to put across new and valid insights into gospel-living in the modern world, while at the same time avoiding the danger of rejecting old ways and introducing change for the sake of change. The balance between the old and the new is sometimes difficult to achieve.

Traditional forms of prayer and devotions do not seem to be relevant to the needs expressed by the young of today; at the same time, these same forms are seen by the elderly to be part and parcel of their spiritual life. To try to satisfy the spiritual needs of a diverse and large community can raise problems which have to be solved for the greater good of all. At each step of the way, we brought decisions and needs to God in prayer. Thus he is able to build up the continuing miracle which is his People, in whom he lives and loves and saves.

Chapter 6

Limehouse Parish Church, St Anne's

London

Christopher Idle

The parish of Limehouse is unusually diverse in its people, and rapidly changing in its profile. It lies two miles east of the City of London's Aldgate boundary; the River Thames flows past its antique warehouses, brand new homes, and a church building dating from 1730—Nicholas Hawksmoor's 'St Anne's'.

After school at Eltham and college at Oxford and Bristol, Christopher Idle began his ministry at Barrow-in-Furness. Since 1968 he and his wife Marjorie (who wrote Joy in the City—*Kingsway, 1988) have worked in inner London: in the East End borough of Tower Hamlets since 1971, and in Limehouse itself since 1976. Their four grown-up sons are currently in Bolivia, Pakistan, Scotland and Limehouse. Christopher's interests include football, jogging, the peace movement and hymns; he has abridged John Wesley's* Journal *and is editor of* Anglican Praise *and the quarterly* News of Hymnody.

'Where are you from?'

'Limehouse, in East London.'

Pause. Then, 'That must be pretty tough.'

The next person to say that is in danger of injury from a large block of Portland stone. Not that I will ever throw it; I don't want to be drummed out of the Fellowship of Reconciliation. More important, we can't spare the Portland stone; we are putting it back on our church building, not taking it off. More of that later.

I would find it very tough being a country vicar with seven congregations; or serving in a suburb, country town, or West End flatland. An all-white church would seem desperately tough, so unlike heaven! If any ministry is not tough, come to that, how can it be biblical? And there are stubborn, thorny, stony scenes in this inner-London borough of Tower Hamlets which may not be quite what the questioner has in mind.

But there is so much more, and so much beauty. The parish of Limehouse features in this book not because it is typical of inner-city work, but because it may illustrate the surprises and the changes in areas which defy our labels. Developers and estate agents may be jumping the gun in recommending 'fashionable Limehouse', but that opening conversation may soon follow a different course.

Last week I walked home a bit down-hearted. I had just managed to avoid a major meeting of an evangelical society in central London, addressed by a Christian leader I much admire. I had also escaped some local Anglicans busy with their incense at the induction of their new vicar. I made two routine calls, and there was old Tom Kitt, sitting on the wall, head in hands.

His brother died last month, and I buried him. Just a handful at the cemetery, but Tom was very touched: 'Just like royalty!' he murmured as we left the graveside in the sunshine. Now he had to live alone after years of companionship which had included the occasional stand-up fight. 'How are you doin'?' he was asking me. 'A bit fed up.'

So we sat together for ten minutes while I regained a sense of proportion. Tom told me to stop rushing about; there was God's word for me that week.

It is easier to think of twenty significant things we have not done than half a dozen that we have. There are huge gaps in our response to the appalling needs of the fairly rich and the quite poor around us. But here we are, and to understand the church we must first look at the parish. Every neighbourhood is unique, precious for its own special qualities; but the pace of change in what is still 'urban priority' Limehouse can be bewildering, its diversity a source of despair, and its wide opportunities a reason for the kind of joy outsiders cannot fathom.

An American consortium plans to build on the Isle of Dogs—half Poplar and half Limehouse—an extension of the City of London's 'square mile' of banks and businesses. Canary Wharf will include the three tallest towers in Europe, 1.5 billion square feet of office space, 50,000 commuting employees and a transformed riverside showpiece. There will be nothing like it in the world.

Even the planning has had deep effects on the psychology of East London, not to mention our existing jobs, roads and trains. Even if the plans are hindered, modified, or delayed, the new Docklands Light Railway—regenerating a stretch of viaduct closed for decades—has started rattling past our windows to provide a city link faster than anything else on wheels.

Limehouse has given birth to a new political party. The 'Limehouse Declaration' launched from Dr. David Owen's Thames-side house announced in 1981 the arrival of the SDP. Five years later the local elections saw the Alliance topple Labour from its traditional power; Mrs Debbie Owen stood at the polling station within the shadow of our church tower, but it was Liberals rather than the Social Democrats who swung the votes.

Within the same patch a hostel for homeless people drew sustained fire from the *Daily Mirror* as a 'Living Hell'.

Once a seamen's hostel with offices and chapel, it became a hotbed of scandal, squalor and frequent fires. Most local people hated it. One changed his mind when he became a Christian; inside were people needing enormous resources of love. And you just never know what will happen; in this building many years ago a young merchant navy cadet heard the call of God in an unforgettable way. The summons was to full-time ministry, and John Hall is now a senior Church of England vicar.

Not all edifices last so long. The least permanent stayed two weeks; another first for Limehouse. Ben Hayden had chosen to live alone in the fall-out shelter he had constructed and stocked, to government specifications, on some waste ground by Limehouse Causeway. I saw big Ben creep in, and fourteen days later I saw him stagger out. He lurched into the arms of a doctor, blinking at the unaccustomed light, before being whisked off on holiday away from the small crowd and the big cameras. Ben was a strong, healthy young man; how would the rest of us cope in a real nuclear disaster, with no back-up team, no waiting cars or medicines, no guarantee that we would not fall sick—or worse—if we were underground?

If 'Ben's bunker' was the most temporary structure, guess whose is the most solid—and the oldest. The Christian church has inherited an architectural masterpiece whose tower weighs 6,000 tons and has dominated road and river—surviving fire, flood and bomb—since the early 1700s.

When a visitor complained that some churches looked like castles and needed only a moat, we pointed out that Limehouse has its own drawbridge—a firm board to take us across when the rainwater overflows the steps. A portcullis might come in handy sometimes.... And another guest commented: 'They didn't just build for posterity; they built for eternity!'

You build for eternity not in stone but with human lives. Who are the people to whom such towers and hostels, homes and bunkers, all belong?

Most still live in rather ordinary flats, from pre-war decay to last year's smartness. Our half-dozen tower-blocks, each housing a village-full of people, will not be repeated. Some strangers find it crowded, but in sixty years the borough has lost three-quarters of its population. That tide is on the turn, but when we mourn the closed churches we must remember that shops, pubs, cinemas and a theatre have all gone too.

The 8,500 souls who live here are not enough to make it an unmanageable unit, nor to justify a second staff member. Vandalism and theft, jammed lifts and sprawling graffiti, strewn rubbish and corrugated iron—all are the familiar marks of urban life, but the poverty is not so desperate or so widespread as on Merseyside or the West Midlands. Joblessness blights many families; the older generation remembers that times were once much harder: happier, they say, but on the bread-line.

The social mix is potentially rich. Chinatown was here; behind the myths of George Formby ('Mr Wu's a window-cleaner now') and Conan Doyle (Lascars, Malays, and opium-dens) lay the reality of a true immigrant and sea-faring community. We have the oldest Chinese restaurants as well as the new up-market style preferred by West End theatre-goers. Limehouse cab-drivers bring them here; Limehouse cooks and waiters feed them.

West Indians came in post-war waves; now they are grandparents, and many black people who cheer the Caribbean cricketers know nothing of the islands at first hand. Nigerians and Ghanaians study law or business management; some decide to settle here. The culture and faith of Bangladesh finds clear expression in the Koranic words above many front doors, and in a gleaming new mosque in a Whitechapel whose original 'chapel' has long gone.

Some differences can be enriching; but many of them harden into divisions. Could we have prevented some local schools dividing along racial lines, from one another or within themselves? Some would not want to; the parents who resent black teachers and vote National Front work for white superiority but hardly exhibit it by their attitudes. Others daub Bengali homes with abuse, or translate their prejudice into arson or violence.

Vietnamese who were once 'boat people' live in flats which look squalid but are gracious inside. (It is easier to send Oxfam a cheque than to make friends with Buddhist neighbours.) They live yards away from the newer, well-heeled boat people who moor their yachts beside Tower Bridge.

'Travellers' (gypsies) descend on open spaces, spreading their cheerful noise and clutter; they sometimes provoke a more bitter response than those from abroad, and working-class East-enders are the most vocal in opposition.

Then there are dossers—an endless stream of vagrants and alcoholics from all parts of Britain. The drug traffic is growing, they say; but it is still the cider-makers and the off-licences who profit most from this human misery. The Salvation Army began in our streets and still runs a men's hostel in Limehouse. Over its garden wall is the Enterprise Zone where new industries spring up and money is no problem. Did I say no problem? It can be the biggest snare of all, and some people weighed down with it are buying their way into the district.

This is our parish. What kind of church could we expect here; what sort of witness should it bear to this local world?

After eleven years in Limehouse we feel as if we have hardly started, but 1976 was a big year for more people than just the new rector. My predecessor retired in 1975. Two of his headaches had been coping with a building without much encouragement, and handling a church merger that failed. A more ritualist congregation had been sewn on to the existing one, but the graft had not taken. The newcomers lost a building and a pastor, and that double bereavement often spells trouble.

There were no takers for the vacant living. *Faith in the*

City says that half the clergy are willing to consider urban priority areas; even this 50 per cent did not stretch their toleration to a shrine with 200 broken windows, and 10 times as many pigeons as people.

After some initial problems, my appointment was finally approved—or rather conceded—because no one else coveted it! And I already belonged to a congregation seeking a home; we had been in Poplar since 1971 and were due for eviction from our much smaller building only half a mile away. For the new merger, then, some had a familiar minister, the others a familiar meeting-place. That gave us hope and helped us face new beginnings; new Bibles, new ways of worship, a new evening service and new friends. Some were lighting candles for the first time; the rest were tasting real bread at the Lord's Supper. Our story since then can never be fully told. Like our church building itself, some parts shine brightly while some need repairs; some will take years to get right, some will stay flawed until all buildings pass away.

Four facts of life

The long and the short

Rectors of Limehouse stay on average for seventeen years; fifteen of us span over two-and-a-half centuries, and I am only the fourth since 1920. Two churchwardens this century served more than thirty years, and even a curate managed eight. There are obvious drawbacks in leaders who stay too long, but it makes the contrast more striking. The mood now is for short-term commitment.

David and Helen, however, are in their third five-year term with the Overseas Missionary Fellowship in Indonesia. Helen was here before I was, and we count them and their children as part of our fellowship too.

Who are today's short-termers? Graduates in their twenties often go abroad for a chosen stint of a year or two; four of our members have done that, but some return early. Back home, lay readers have not stayed long; one licensed reader lasted barely two years, another three. Many office-bearers think in that timescale.

For some jobs this is clearly right. A churchwarden who needs a break as family commitments change, a gifted student who belongs to us until finals, someone whose firm moves on—all these make valued contributions. But when this trend is the norm it affects all our thinking. 'New' ideas emerge four times in a decade and it is discouraging if older members say, 'We tried that two years ago.' Or a new leader initiates a project without staying to see it through growth, adaptation, crisis or conclusion. We miss a longer perspective on particular families and it tends to be the incomers who move on, not those native to East London. They have their farewells, thanks and presentations; but does not the key to growth lie elsewhere?

Strings and pipe

The gifts and limitations in our music affect all of our worship. Our organ is magnificent; our musicians have also been skilled at the piano, guitar and wind instruments. We have laboured for the big occasions and been lifted by the flowing sounds. But what happens afterwards? Without much continuity, it takes another struggle to create a group for the next event. Why can't it happen regularly? Time is part of the answer; this is nobody's number one priority. We do not worship the keyboard; praise is not the key to everything, and I am not persuaded by Liberace theology. But should we be praying, let alone paying, for a music director?

Sticks and stones

By any standards our church building is remarkable. Architectural historian Sir John Summerson, who likes it, calls it 'a shocker'. It held 2,500 for one historic wedding, and morning and evening congregations of 1,000; but that was during the 1860s and 70s, half way through its life to date. For the rest of the time, many pews have been dusted, polished, and empty. Had it been a Victorian barn instead of a Georgian treasure, it would have been abandoned long ago.

Any rector here, like his Spitalfields counterpart, is in danger of being 'seduced by the building'. In spite of its shape, size, temperature, and cost; in spite of the inevitable restoration appeal; in spite of gutters and pipes, boilers and birds, reports and committees—one gets to love it. Its main-road (A13) position attracts strangers every week, and bears witness to the Christians who live here, and to the faith we cling to and dare to proclaim. Our GLC-funded notice-boards say 'Jesus Christ is Lord'; and no one knows how much a parish church means to its half-believing neighbours until it is demolished. With one Roman Catholic exception, it is the last surviving church building in Limehouse, as it was one of the first. We may even regain the priority of the preaching for which it was built, and gently minimise the Victorian 'vandalism' that erected a high altar and other anachronisms. Ultimately the building is neither eternal nor essential, but to let it fall would be the crowning act of folly in a place which has seen rubble and wreckers enough. I am called not to malign it but to use it thankfully while it stands.

Buildings alone neither attract the unwilling nor deter the determined; but they can make life easier or harder. When our current scheme opened a crypt room, providing warmth, conversation and coffee after most services—the average attendance rose by 10 per cent and stayed up. And it is proving a marvellous place for meals together.

Buildings also attract thieves, vandals and policemen. These last from a headquarters which has smashed some notorious murder gangs, have so far caught two sets of trespassing small boys. Somehow the lead, brass, pictures and clocks all sneak off unhindered—the grandfather clock wrapped tastefully in a surplice. But the police are ever ready to arrest anyone legitimately employed on the fabric. They accosted me and a visiting missionary removing a broken notice-board, a young man mending a window, and my son as he applied graffiti-remover to the porch stonework. One day they will apprehend a bona fide burglar.

Women and children first?

Our membership reflects the numerical predominance of women in the church, but not dramatically. As it happens, our women's group has just folded up; forty of our ninety members are men. A boy baby-boom is working its way through Climbers and Explorers, and our evening congregation is largely male. Equal members of men and women attend our four mid-week groups—just over twenty of each, though the women are more consistent. The confirmation register shows that in ten years, twenty-five men have been confirmed, and only eighteen women. During that time we raised the lower limit to fourteen years; over half the total were at least in their twenties. So the men are holding their own. But our pensioners are mostly female; and West Indian males do not commit themselves much beyond Sundays.

We find that morning congregations grow while the evening falters. At 10.30 our thirty-five adults have risen to nearly sixty, while the number of children stays between twenty and thirty; many of these have Christian parents, and we have a good team of nine leaders for the junior groups. At night the loss of a choir meant a decline from nearly forty to below thirty, but the proportion of adults has increased.

Four false starts

The Pastoral Team

Bright ideas sometimes come on holidays, or as I jog, read or pray; sometimes they come from others. The pastoral team was a holiday idea; when I am not pressed down by daily commitments, larger planning can take shape.

In 1978 we had failed to find any replacement for Wendy, our parish worker who had left the previous autumn and died, tragically yet triumphantly, a few months later. Was God telling us not to look for a 'professional', but to recognise the talent we already had? Among us were several people (all men, as it happened) with considerable training and experience between them. So we began to meet, read, pray, think and plan together. One or two came and went; but when four years later we were down to two, the experiment ended.

I should have looked less at qualifications and more at gifts. We should have written down what kind of commitment we expected from one another. We should have been more honest, however painful it was. We had encouragement from two successive area deans and bishops; but in the end we were indulging ourselves, not enabling the church to grow. Few people who stayed a month among us could have guessed which of our members made up the team.

Teenagers

The confirmation figures quoted earlier may seem tiny, even more so when we add that in fifteen years, no sixteen to nineteen-year-old was confirmed. They are caught early (twelve to fourteen, and one of fifteen) or join later. Here is a yawning gap in our ministry.

If it has even proved tricky to keep going a club night for the younger teenagers who join in on Sundays; our efforts to meet those who do not join in have certainly foundered. Not that we ever planned any open youth work; should we have done? With three different groups of street-roaming kids we opened up for evenings of fairly low-key entertainment; some still hung around the usual table-games, but concentration was often too short even for these. There have been moments of wonder when we talked spontaneously about Christ; but nothing permanent has come, and after a few weeks the youngsters are off again.

Even in a gifted church, the skills that might help disadvantaged teenagers and the time to spend with them are severely limited. A solid core of the church finds it hard to relate to these occasional disturbers of worship and destroyers of furniture; an open group never justifies itself in measurable statistics, and all that surfaces is the repair-bill after they have left us. But they hold their place in the hearts and prayers of some of us.

Unholy baptism

A different source of strain lies in the realm of Christian initiation. Baptisms have dropped from fifty a year to five; but I do not count that as failure! Even some of the survivors slip through our fairly tight policy. The cost of insisting that the parents of an infant candidate have some glimmering of what it means to follow Christ is that in almost every block we meet someone who says 'St Anne's? Not likely; they wouldn't christen our baby.' It doesn't make door-to-door evangelism any easier; it is the church's reward for generations of conniving in the superstition that all babies must be 'done'. We preach justification by faith;

we have practised justification *solo baptismo*—by baptism alone, with no faith attached. That is a false start.

I long to show how the sacrament ought to work, with full-blooded baptisms among the flock; but some Christian families see the travesty we have made of it and want nothing like that for their children. So the pagans want baptism on demand; the faithful settle for 'Thanksgiving' or nothing.

But we do have our happier times: the West Africans who appear on every page of the register with their annual child; the Welsh nurse who was baptised by immersion in the sea on our summer outing; and the ordinand's wife who rushed to the front one Sunday, with the first hymn for their baby's ceremony already overdue, and said, 'You're not going to believe this, Chris, but one of the godfathers has locked himself in the toilet.'

Church and school

The education offered by our 'Church of England Aided' school, with a little bit of help from the church, is hardly a failure. We have been privileged in our headteachers, some equally good deputies and other staff, and in having four school families who are active church members. If that seems few in a complete infant and junior school, it is better than the time when our own two youngest boys were the only pupils we saw on Sundays. One teacher belongs to our church—one more than when we arrived.

If there are unfulfilled dreams, they lie partly in the gap between most parents and most of the church, and our inability to bridge it. Some parents who are uncomfortable with Asian or even West Indian company seek admission for their children. 'Don't get me wrong; I'm not racist—far from it. But let's face it; this is what you might call a white school, and that's what I want!'

Another false start. It isn't all white; nor, certainly, are its Christian families. But it tends that way. It certainly isn't all Christian; that would pose different problems. But whether from the flood of Inner London Education Authority documents, the occasional threat of 'industrial action' (which our teachers generally avoid), the status and scope of religious education, or the pastoral care of the whole school—there are still too many question-marks around for our peace of mind.

Four frustrations

Prior claims

I do not rule the people with a rod of iron; they wouldn't let me. I am delighted when Christians widen their horizons beyond the parochial and the religious. But people sing the refrain repeatedly, 'I'm sorry I won't be there, but somewhere else instead.' If they are sorry, at least they feel the tension. But the unspoken assumption is that the local church comes second, or holds some lower spot on their list of priorities: 'Friends came round ... The dog was sick ... It was so wet ... Something turned up!'

This must happen in every church. I cannot judge which competing claims are truly vital. We are not overburdened with meetings; when we try to reduce the 'churchy' evenings, I am still surprised at how eagerly the gaps are plugged with yet more. But where the church is embattled, the stakes high and the warfare uncertain, I long for more of the saints to say 'Come hell or high water, I'll be there!' I have to, don't I?

Pious diversions

London has a further set of attractions which make it a place of luxurious choice for Christians. Those who succumb to them feel no need to apologise to their local church; it is enough that the transatlantic 'personality' is in town, the crusade teach-in has arrived, the gospel film is being shown. Javanese villagers face no such temptations.

If the local pastor is also keen, he faces the job of completing the form, enthusing the fellowship, booking the coach, and sending the cheque. We are learning to ask, 'Will this, in the long-term, help to build the church of Jesus Christ in our area?' There are few loyalties beyond this one.

The big meeting may help. It supplies a sense of the size of the church in a way that we cannot: a sharing of other traditions, other styles and other songs. Our links with three nearby Baptist churches have provided much encouragement on a smaller scale in prayer, praise, witness and protest.

But when we are into the thousands, we trail back home feeling a bit flattened by our own sheer ordinariness. We can't reproduce the band and the choir that got them all singing. Those healings and conversions we heard about— why aren't they happening here? I no longer feel diminished by it all; I know that my dear friends and their entertainers have missed the point. It's what happens locally that counts. But they have to see it for themselves.

False divisions

I describe myself as 'full-time'; I could have said 'trained' or simply 'paid'. That is another way of expressing the two classes in our church; me—and everyone else! Their account of our growth would be different from mine. This is not the place to explore the history of the clergy/laity divide; but here and there it hurts. Who cares if I fail; who dares tell me? Who knows what I do all day? If people did, the church's demands on me would be different: dramatically reduced ('No one came to see me'), or excitingly increased ('Can you explain what Christians believe?').

It hurts when I send out 'help' signals that are not picked up, or when I am more explicit and then misunderstood; when I achieve something difficult and special, and nobody notices!

There are glorious exceptions to this gloomy list; often quite unexpected. But what matters to me sometimes doesn't seem to matter to anyone else. Let one major example conclude this quartet.

Who cares for the city?

When it comes to visiting every home, at Christmas or for Mission to London, our record is not bad. With or without me, a group of brave and nervous souls pray by the bookstall, going out into the chilly evening in twos and threes to tell the parish we're in business.

But when it comes to getting stuck in to some crying social needs, I miss my Christian friends. Even if evangelism were the only yardstick, it would seem a good idea to make friends with non-Christians at a level of common concern. Some members are heroes in that respect. But again, the issue of race seems too alarming for most.

This borough has not seen incidents as terrifying in scale as those elsewhere, but our lesser offences are ugly enough. Bishop Jim Thompson of Stepney pioneered a group working for justice which became the Tower Hamlets Association for Racial Equality (THARE). My membership is more than nominal, but only just. Local clergy turn up for meetings and action, but Christian laypeople are very few. Is that due to a history of 'heroic' clergy encouraging a passive laity, or a theology of 'Father knows best'?

The first Limehouse festival held in and around our church premises found many Christians running for cover rather than rising to the occasion; it was left to Ben (of the bunker) to mastermind music, food, and much else. We did better at the second festival; now a third is being planned. But why do we meet to pray for the sick if no one ever visits George, who has spent six years in a psychiatric ward a mile away? It could be a thousand miles; but George is a Christian. And there are community anxieties over docks and roads where Christians could play a key role. We clearly don't agree about priorities and diversions! But now let's turn to happier things.

Many fulfilments

There are far more than four on this list. These are some of the joys of the Limehouse square mile and today's church which God has planted.

The mixture

Few local groups combine such varied shades of colour, class and culture as the church. We took a photo of ourselves to give to Anesta as she left for retirement in St Lucia. It is still the best way of answering the question 'What sort of congregation do you get?' Not the best way of asking it; but I never tire of telling of the work of grace in so many whose diverse faces looked up into John's camera that Sunday.

Young adults

I remember the first time a nurse joined us. We never became an adjunct of the London Hospital Christian Fellowship—I have addressed it twice in sixteen years—but the trickle of nurses, medics and other students has steadily grown. We thought of gathering this 'hospital group' together, but it seemed better to include the whole age-range. The result was the eighteen-to-thirty group—a regular gathering of friends which has not taken the world by storm, sometimes lost its way, rarely reached a dozen in all, yet which has given much support and inspiration to those (mainly singles) passing through college, or a London job, or just at that particular stage of life.

They include problems too—the fast-talking newcomers who think their academic training makes them a godsend to the less educated. But those who value the privilege of inner-city church membership need humility and realism, silence and self-denial, and the ability to make friends of people unlike themselves and of different ages. They understand the scale of things for bustravellers and non-drivers, for whom two miles is a long way. The best of them do not come to take over, but to serve. And the fitter ones prove vital when we stage our own sponsored marathons—twenty-six miles is a fair stretch.

Wednesday nights

Sundays excepted, nothing has excited me more than 7.45 to 9.45 on Wednesday. We come to hear God's word and to pray; the setting may be a cup of tea, biscuits and crumbs, babies, cats and dogs, and shared news. As long as the frame doesn't obscure the picture, it serves to set it off.

There are other times for gossip; the priceless excellence of Wednesday is the wealth of the Scriptures, looked at reverently and interpreted by a great variety of people. Most who lead wish they had prepared better; many could lead more firmly if they had more confidence; all of them help us to see in a Gospel, a Letter or a Psalm things we never saw before. In all, sixteen different homes have opened for these evenings; since 1985 we have met in four groups who come together from time to time so that in growing more intimate we do not grow apart. And we sing more then, too.

The study-outline is usually home-made; most people like a brief sheet of questions, and half the church members take part. Each group has its own flavour, but none is homogeneous; accountants learn from hostel-dwellers, the secure from the lonely, the strong and silent from the disturbed or unemployed, and vice versa! When I cannot be there, I miss it more than anything else.

Tales of the unexpected

When a domestic crisis interrupts a study-session, it can do wonders for our prayers. The unexpected demands or offers can be humbling or frightening to a minister. But the gospel we are entrusted with is well able to cope with every situation—starting with ourselves.

When an East-end temper flares, a Christian fellow-worker can storm out and vow never to return. He'll be back, almost always; and such explosions are soon forgotten. When East-end love overflows, the generosity of a brother or sister can be breathtaking.

And every neighbour can teach us something. Michael was a six-foot-six African squatting in the next-door flats. He bought a Bible and studied the charts at the back. On Sunday he strode into church, robes billowing, and began to declaim from the front: Allah and Jehovah are one, he said, and God had called him to lead a world-wide revival uniting Islam and Christianity. He was escorted out. A month later he was fined 50p for pouring a can of Coke over a policeman's trousers in the Mile End Road.

Death

If baptisms are frustrating and weddings fruitless, funerals often bring someone's deepest concerns to the surface, for a time. The death of a Christian is a glorious opening to explain publicly to friends and family how the gospel of Christ worked for the one whose earthly body lies in the coffin before us. When we are warned, the weeks before death can be rich as well as painful; if it is sudden, the months afterwards bring their own healing ministries as well as grief.

Morning prayer

Nearly every day Limehouse hears the chiming of our solitary bell high above the traffic of the growing rush-hour. Time to unlock and pray, according to the law of the Church of England. Evenings are not so canonically observed; but 7.30 am is about right for twenty minutes of quiet, even if I am alone.

I have abandoned the already tired language of the 'modern' service, returning to the Book of Common Prayer. When I am lost for other words, here at least are Psalms, Collects, and 'Our Father...'; on other days, and when someone joins me, we use much more of it.

It was a weekly visitor (a diplomat) who persuaded me that if he preferred '1662' and so did I, we might as well use it—whatever other texts we have on Sundays. At different times, scores of others have dropped in to make it a 'two or three gathered together', rather than just one with the angels.

Consecutive Bible-reading is our nourishment; our intercession is sparked by the church's monthly prayer diary, and by my own heart-cries of the day: 'Lord, thank you... Lord, please... Lord, help!'

Family

In celebrating the church 'family' we do not ignore the single or the separated, the widowed or divorced. But there is also the human nuclear family, honoured rather than put down by the words of Christ about brothers and sisters. Our church includes one three-generation family, and three families where the second generation is adult. One or two more will qualify if they persevere!

One of the three is my own: Marjorie and our four sons, who all share the ministry—sometimes too much, but it is hard to picture it otherwise. When we moved from Poplar the boys were twelve, eleven, nine and six. As far as we could grasp it, we agreed to battle together as one team. We argue, sometimes hotly, and the fate of the sermon over Sunday lunch is hilarious or horrific— but always helpful. The loyalty and labour of those living under the same roof is beyond price; when they are the target for attack, the pain is especially sharp. Thank you, God; without them I would fold up.

Preaching

If I have left to last the ministry of the word, it is not as a postscript but as the crown. In church and out, we do some strange and wonderful things 'for the sake of the gospel'; but there is no substitute for God's messenger declaring and applying his message—Bible-based, Spirit-led, Christ-centred. This is my calling, and by this we stand or fall. The soil and the seed were made for each other: and though the ground seems tough, the seed is dynamic:

So strong, and yet so weak,
the church of Christ shall speak;
his cross our greatest need,
his word the vital seed
that brings a fruitful harvest.[1]

Note

[1] Quoted from *Hymns for Today's Church*, with grateful acknowledgement.

Chapter 7

Aston Parish Church
Ss Peter and Paul, Birmingham

John Holden

The enormous red sandstone structure of Aston Parish Church stands less than a hundred yards from Aston Villa Football Club, and, close by, a loop of the A38(M) arches almost over the roof. Opposite, the spacious green of Aston Park and ornate turrets of Aston Hall belie the urban setting, for only a few yards away stretches a row of condemned housing. A hypermarket and a plot of rubbish-strewn land complete this strange blend of grandeur and decay.

Aston Parish houses 10,000 people in high-rises and council estates—40 per cent of them out of work—where once there were 25,000 in a thriving industrial community. Here John and Helga Holden came in 1975 with their daughters Ann and Catherine (both now doctors). They found a dwindling but faithful congregation. Now—since God moved the Holdens on in 1987—John has left behind him a church expanded in numbers, but, of equal importance, one fired by a vision for mission, a neighbourhood church of both black and white families. 'Helga has very much been a partner in this,' he says. 'As a family we've kept each other going.' This chapter, then, tells the Holdens' story—from mission in Uganda to mission in Aston.

It was 4th June 1975 and around 5.30 pm. Helga and I had just crossed from Kenya to the border control on the Ugandan side. The passport officer sat there silently and, looking embarrassed, handed me a deportation order. He suggested I walk the half mile across the border divide, back to Kenya. My first thought was, 'I'm not going voluntarily; it would look like giving up.' Helga's first thought was 'CMS will have to pay the air fare for me!' If I was to be deported, we decided we had to let the Ugandans do it. I had stood by others as they were deported, even going with them into the dreaded CID headquarters in Kampala.

When the CID came they took me and my car to Tororo police station, where they told me to lie on the concrete floor. Next day we left before 6.00 am and drove non-stop, 200 miles to Kampala. I was put in a cell with a Muslim—an Ethiopian refugee. How ironic and tragic that this man's hope lay in political asylum in Amin's Uganda at the height of his reign of terror! Such can be the choice in Africa. I was the fortunate one. Within twenty-four hours I was put on a plane to Nairobi, on my way to London. From the time I received the deportation order until I arrived at my parents' home in Lancashire, fewer than forty-eight hours had passed! Helga had packed and followed eight days later, declining the CID officer's offer that she might stay, since 'only your husband is deported'.

First impressions

A long-held conviction that a main frontier of mission in this country is the inner city was now put to the test! Also to be tested was the need for a long-term commitment to such areas. These are my first impressions on being invited to consider Aston Parish Church. One churchwarden and the

PCC secretary had already indicated they were resigning at the next AGM. In fact they had only stayed on at the last AGM because the previous vicar had got his resignation in first! Morale in the community and the church was at a very low ebb. The church was dirty and numbers had dwindled. The outgoing incumbent and two priests in charge of the neighbouring parish in Aston (St James) had written a paper which was shown me on my visit. It logically argued why no attempt should be made to revive mission and ministry based on the parish church—and advised walking away from the building and starting in an appropriately built small church centre. I thought there were some fundamental questions begged in this paper. One of the co-writers, years later, said he had been proved wrong.

At my first parochial church council meetings, I discovered just how low morale among the congregation was. After outlining some ideas, aims and hopes, including growth in the spirit of worship, one of the keenest members looked at me and said, 'When they've (congregation and local people) had a look at you, and you are down to six people sitting in the choir stalls for Evensong, what are you going to do then?'

Helga and I said our prayers and asked God to show us clearly if this was the place where he wanted us to give the best years of our lives. He showed us very clearly from signs and his word that it was. And so we came to Aston. What hit me, and I remember it vividly, was that within days I was promised a breakdown in my health, my marriage, my faith... I would go to drink or simply leave the ministry altogether! This was heavy pressure, because it came mostly from clergy, whose experience anyone would be foolish to ignore. The main effect was to make me more cautious than I might have been, but it also confirmed for me the priority to be faithful in prayer. I now know that of twenty-eight incumbents who served in Aston deanery in the fifteen years to 1987, over half have suffered one or more of the fates I was promised.

What did we find? A dwindling congregation dispirited and shell-shocked by the so-called redevelopment of Aston. But also, one has to remember that most churches like Aston Parish Church had had regular congregations of anything from 400 to 1,000 people in the post-war years up to the late 1950s. In the space of little more than ten years, church attendance at Aston had fallen to a fifth, sometimes less than 10 per cent of what it had been! Although the stuffing had been knocked out of the congregation, just as it had been out of the wider community and other local churches, nonetheless I found a nucleus of people committed to serving Christ and offering their talents. An indication of this was that they ran a stewardship campaign during the interregnum. That took faith and guts. But first let us look at the historical background of the parish.

Looking back

The Domesday Book (1086) testifies that the gospel has been proclaimed in Aston for 900 years. Incidentally, it rated Aston at 75 shillings, three times that of Birmingham! It records the presence of a resident priest. Following this evidence of a Saxon church come other records which show the building of a Norman church. Another reminder of continuity is part of a thirteenth-century preaching-cross in the present church. The Norman church was considerably enlarged in the 1880s doubling the seating capacity. In fact almost all except the fifteenth-century tower and spire was replaced.

The then vicar saw that his parish of 35,000 to 40,000 was divided into 6 areas by a river, canals, railway lines, large factories and major arterial roads. So after rebuilding and enlarging the church in 1880, in the best of Victorian tradition he set about building six daughter churches or mission halls. He took on eleven staff, including curates, a secretary, Church Army evangelist, a parish nurse and a full-time clerk-cum-verger. Team ministry is not new!

One of these six daughter churches became a separate parish (St Martin's, Perry Common). Of the remaining five, three were closed and two compulsorily purchased through redevelopment. Dyson Hall, the last and most well known, closed in 1975 having served thousands of people in countless ways for eighty years. The 'Dyson' part of the parish was one of the last areas of Birmingham to be cleared for industrial use. A community is effectively assassinated in the name of development! The bulldozer had already done its work, cutting a swathe through the parish to create space for the Aston expressway—a seven-lane motorway providing the primary access to the city from the M6 (Spaghetti Junction). Bereft of a church hall, part of the north aisle in the parish church had been converted into a lounge for meetings and limited social purposes. Without this facility, it is probable that the church building would have deteriorated and become completely unusable. As it was, all except one window was broken on the north side, as were some of the east windows. Adhesive carpet binding could not keep out the weather. Sufficient rain and dirt still blew in to defeat the efforts of a cleaner working five mornings a week! Finances had also deteriorated and by the end of 1975 the cleaner was asked to find alternative work. The parish could not afford to pay her!

On my arrival, the treasurer handed me a list of unpaid bills which, adjusted for inflation, totalled nearly £10,000. Three firms were taking us to court for non-payment. We were overdrawn on current account. After being Vicar for three months I discovered that the church was also in debt on capital account by an even larger amount.

By 1975, many of those who worshipped at the parish church had previously been members of one of the mission halls or daughter churches. It was they who had much of the drive and instinct for things, though lacking the opportunities to exercise leadership. Their background meant they had experienced generations of clergy who rarely understood the industrial areas. In living memory, the parish church had been almost totally 'pew rented'—so had no place for the poor. It had been made clear that their place was in mission halls! Of course, few Church of England clergy had experience of working-class areas before training, and rarely received any during it.

People remembered the numbers of those taking Bible study notes being between 300 and 400. There was no list by 1975. But there was a thriving Sunday school—amazing, as most inner-city churches had given up years earlier. It was led by Ron Morris, an ex-Boys' Brigade captain, who held on. Many of the remaining 'eclectic' members of the congregation harboured lingering assumptions of 'Get the right vicar and a robed choir and we shall return to days of glory'! The choir had disbanded in 1970 and there was no organist when I arrived.

I came prepared to preside over the closure of this historic parish church, but by God's grace, to pray and apply lessons and principles of mission for a minimum of ten years and leave the rest to God. Uganda was a good preparation.

'The Church of England has never really had a working-class constituency.' Robert Runcie acknowledged this when interviewed just before his enthronement in 1980!

I did not expect to do in 10 years, or at all, what the whole Church of England had not done in 200 years since the Industrial Revolution. But I believed the grace of God sufficient to sustain us in our calling. Four years in Uganda had confirmed that, whatever the outcome.

The heart of the matter

At the heart of effective mission—wherever it is—are belief in the Lord Jesus and the conviction that God has called us to be in that particular place: knowledge that this is where the Holy Spirit has guided us. When we left Uganda, we thought and prayed hard about where God wanted us to be, and we believe that Aston was indeed the place. As time passed, for we were convinced it was important to make a long-term commitment to our mission, it was this conviction that sustained us.

We didn't see our coming here as a complete break from the work we had been doing in Uganda. On the contrary, we wanted to sustain that link. As Simon Barrington-Ward, General Secretary of CMS, once put it, 'One thing is clear. If we can really come together for mission within our own country, we shall certainly be more effective in doing so across the world. Those committed to the one movement must surely be committed to the other.'[1]

Thus, immediately I came to the diocese, the local CMS executive committee asked me to serve on it, and CMS in London asked me to be a member of the national CMS Home Members' Committee, quite a large body consisting of a diverse group of Christians from across Britain with experience in mission both at home and abroad. Also, since I was a close friend of the new principal of CMS training college, Crowther Hall (in Selly Oak, Birmingham), he proposed that we arrange for students of Crowther to spend half a day each week in Aston to earth their missionary training in the realities of the inner city. For twelve years then, we had fifty or sixty missionaries here, helping to prepare them for mission overseas.

In 1979 I wrote an open letter to CMS suggesting that CMS was being called by God to put some of its resources and people into the inner city as a frontier for mission. In itself that letter and its results warrants a whole chapter! Not having the space to tell the whole story here, I can at least say that one of the results for the parish was the arrival of a CMS mission partner in the parish—Martin Young with his wife Suzette and two children, who sold their home in London and came to live in one of our high-rise blocks.

Hearts and hands together

My colleagues and I in Aston have been not so much
teachers as workers and trainers, concerned with the principles of mission and, even more, with their application.
Though I've occasionally lectured at Selly Oak, I believe
that if I have any gift, it's in relating the gospel to the situation in which I find myself. For all of us in the parish, then,
came some big and searching questions: What does it mean
to be a Christian in Aston? What does it mean to live in a
high-rise, to be unemployed, or to be working three shifts?
What does it mean to be a Christian from the Caribbean,
essentially unwelcomed by the Christian community on arrival?

Birmingham is the second city of England, the 'city of a
thousand trades' as we call it. The city is heavily industrialised, and people in working class areas have been
largely estranged from the gospel and the church. We have
never truly won them for Christ. Picture a clergyman in any
factory in Birmingham walking out onto the shop floor in
his clerical collar. Everyone recognises him. The average
worker would conclude that he had come to ask for some
help or money, or else to bring bad news, or perhaps even
that he had lost his bearings! This scene shows us the
breadth of the gap between alienated working people and
the church; it is an indictment of the church.

Light years apart?

How do we begin to bridge that gap? This is where the industrial chaplaincy comes in; the ordained minister actually
gives some time to go to people in their work place. The
truth is that even in the days when (like Aston) parishes
were staffed with as many as ten curates who spent forty

hours a week visiting, the church rarely met ordinary working people. Evening visits were limited, except before baptisms or weddings. Christians were not going to where people *were*.

Long before I was in the ordained ministry, I worked as an apprentice at Rolls Royce in Crewe, and later as an accountant at Lucas Limited, whose original factory was on Great Kings Street in Birmingham. Those years were—I'm convinced—as important a preparation for ministry as any formal theological training I had later at Ridley Hall. Lucas is a household name in Birmingham, manufacturing car electrical components. When I came here as vicar and joined the industrial chaplains' team, I was asked to be industrial chaplain to Lucas. This meant that I spent at least half a day a week meeting people on the shop floor and in their offices. Sadly, the main factory on Kings Street has been closing over the last few years, and many of its component factories have been sold off; it's one of Birmingham's dying companies now.

We can have no stereotypes in our evangelism here. It isn't adequate to say, 'These are our methods of evangelism, and all we have to do is punch it out from the pulpit.' Instead, we have to be open to the guiding of the Spirit; our evangelism has to be rooted in the reality of the inner city, with a commitment to discovering the Holy Spirit's way of working effectively within that context. At the same time that we respond to the commission of Christ in Matthew Chapter 28 to make disciples, we must remember the second part of that commission: to teach all that Jesus has commanded us to obey. By going to visit people in their work place, we are confronted by the question of what it means to be a Christian on the shop floor. If there is irresponsible trade union action; if people are moderate but are entrapped by hardline union activity—how then do they live out their Christianity? We can only learn by being *with* people in the situation. Surely it is tragic that in most churches' intercessions there is invariably only oblique (if any) reference to the world of work; that there is barely adequate preparation in some theological colleges for any understanding of an industrial worker's life.

As my colleagues and I visited people in their homes during times of bereavement or celebration, they soon discovered whether or not we had a feel for their lives. Without that, we could not bridge the distance between church and people. What *does* it mean to be a factory worker with fifty-one years of experience on the shop floor? How then (to take just one example) can the church minister effectively at such a man's funeral?

Charlie

A couple of years after I started to visit Lucas, Charlie, one of the toolmakers, died. He was unmarried, in his late fifties, without any relatives. I took the funeral, and the management let the thirty or forty people from the tool room leave their work to come to the funeral. They were the only people there, and I suppose it could have been a gloomy, bitter occasion. Instead, as I related Charlie's life to Scripture, everything came alive.

Very simply, in thanking God for Charlie, I spoke about how all his work had gone into making tools that enabled the manufacture of car components, which in their turn enabled and enriched all our lives—yours and mine. Where would we be without transport? It enhances our life. Indirectly, all of us—millions of people over the years—have received a little bit of Charlie. We cannot assert, then, that our salary cheques or weekly pay packets are what enrich our lives; instead it is the service of others that goes on week in and week out, a service we hardly ever stop to think about. And as I preached that day, I realised afresh that under God I was helping people to move towards God through their growing understanding that the gospel *was* relevant to their lives. Needless to say, I was in the process of learning a lot about obedience myself!

Birmingham and Jinja

This idea—that it was important to relate the gospel to the local situation—didn't have to be sold to Aston Parish Church. In fact, when I arrived, there was deep frustration and sometimes real anger among the loyal congregation towards the ordained ministry, even though my predecessors had been sincerely devoted to serving the parish. I'm not an academic, so humanly speaking the thought of my having responsibility for fitting other young clergy for ministry was absurd. In Uganda, however, we had been living in the industrial city of Jinja, ministering to both Roman Catholics and Anglicans, and we started a joint course offering orientation to industrial life. Young men who were training for the Catholic priesthood and other students training to be pastors in the Church of Uganda came to Jinja, where they spent time doing unskilled manual labour in local factories: copper smelting and cotton factories and steel mills.

Our experience in Jinja convinced me that Aston was an ideal setting to engage in similar ministry. I confess I was very hesitant when I floated the idea to Ridley Hall, Cambridge, where I had trained, but—as it turned out—the Lord's timing was evident, and my hesitancy proved unjustified. The Advisory Council for the Church's Ministry was at the same time just about to introduce into the official examinations a pastoral studies paper. Thus when I offered to train students here, Ridley jumped at the offer; my first long-term curate was among the initial six who came on the course in 1978. In the words of the principal of Ridley (and over the years at least forty students have come and gone), this course was one of the most 'informative and helpful' things Ridley has done in preparing its students for ministry.

Local families in the congregation offered accommodation to the students; almost all of them were staying in small terraced houses. In one instance a young woman from Wesley House in Cambridge training for the Methodist ministry stayed with Ray and Zelda and their daughter Clare. They have two bedrooms, and the only way to the bathroom is through the second bedroom. Clare gave up her bed and slept on the sofa for five weeks so that the student could have her bedroom. This student worked in the kitchens at Lucas—a complete eye opener!—and through both work and home had a full orientation on how the people of Aston actually live.

Confronting the realities of living the gospel in such a place proved painful for some. Four out of forty students who came on the course did not go forward eventually to be ordained. I know that at least two of the four would have gone forward to ordination if they had not come to Aston— and would have given up or burned out of their ministry within the first few years. But those who stayed the course have written back later of the great encouragement it has been. The inner city in all its strangeness might have been a threat; instead, it has helped them see how they can win people to Christ, showing others that the gospel *is* relevant to their lives. They *have* seen how they can meet others where they are; they *have* seen what it means to be black in Birmingham, to live in a high-rise. The gospel, they have found, has something to say both as a resource and as a place of fellowship in the church.

Knit together

The integration of the gospel with daily life goes hand in hand with the worship of God, with what we pray, teach and preach about. When we're training lay people, even for something as simple as assisting at Communion, it's not the mechanics that count. We have to stress that what does count is receiving the life of Christ together, and living out that life in the factory and high-rise. Some of the lay people we've trained have been at best nervous about reading the prayers in front of others, and at worst unable to read a single line of a hymn. Still, God has used them to enrich our worship deeply. We have all been lifted up by them.

This sharing in worship has not come quickly. Informal house groups did not come together for a long time after we arrived in Aston. The pattern of groups meeting in homes is in fact a middle-class one; whereas middle-class folk deliberately arrange to meet in groups, people in Aston were used to dropping in and out of each other's homes in a casual one-to-one fashion. After all, there's not much space in a terraced house, and with children in small rooms, and the parents in and out on shifts, there simply aren't the facilities.

We began gently with a series of carefully planned Lent groups in the church itself. As people saw the benefits of small groups, we moved out into homes. The whole process took four or five years.

Here we took up again the question of what it means to be a Christian in Aston, what needs we should be meeting locally as a body of believers. Out of these groups came the realisation that we needed a second-hand clothes shop and an advice or drop-in centre. As a result, we opened a community centre in 1980 to house both, as well as a pre-school playgroup, a good neighbours' club for the elderly, and a men's club.

Out of these groups, too, came specific and practical prayer needs. In one instance moderate trade union members in one factory reported that some of their colleagues in a local brewery were taking bribes to find people jobs. They wanted prayer to know how to deal with the situation, and once again the gospel was relevant.

Another group that arose from lay leadership towards the end of my time in Aston was a men's group. We had prayed and moved in this direction ever since 1980, and when the group first met in 1987, fifteen men came along.

The aim was to provide monthly social, fellowship and spiritual support for those who attended, and the setting was a natural one in which men could befriend each other and share in the life of Christ.

Healing hands

At Ridley I had imagined that healing was given to individuals; then we had a visit from a Nigerian pastor. He soon convinced me that healing is not just a gift to individuals but to the church. Through his teaching, and through my own prayers, I became quite convinced of this truth. Later, as a curate, though I found little response to my ideas of healing, I always asked a small group to pray for me if I had a special visit to make. On one occasion I was called to the intensive care unit of the hospital to comfort a woman who even with drugs could not cope with the severe pain she was suffering. She was healed then and there of her pain.

In all lay ministry, healing should be a natural part of the work of the church. At Aston when I first arrived no one had heard of the practice of the healing ministry in an ordinary Anglican congregation. It was a joy over the years to see many people involved. First we encouraged small groups to go out and observe the healing ministry in other denominations in Birmingham. Then very slowly after four or five years we were able to hold our first healing service on a Sunday, with Communion. About thirty-five people came forward for the laying on of hands, which we administered as a church in two's and three's, having prayed and met together beforehand. We saw specific healings in services and in people's homes.

One healing that authenticated the lay ministry as far as I'm concerned was my own! For some time I'd suffered from a trapped nerve in my neck that resulted in severe pain down one arm; I began to wear a clumsy, heavy collar round my neck and to go to physiotherapy. Neither helped.

So I came for prayer and the laying on of hands, and over about four months was completely healed.

Ray and Zelda's daughter Clare was another who was healed. In her case the healing was not physical so much as emotional. Various events in her childhood had left her deeply scarred, but healing prayer transformed her over several years. She is now a lovely, radiant young woman, no longer the broken person of before. Once again, the gospel met her where she was!

It starts on our knees

Before I wrote this chapter, I asked two people, without warning, what they would point at as being most significant in the life of Aston Parish Church. One came back immediately with a detailed list of both primary and secondary things that meant much to her in the life of church. The other, Steve, came back some time later and simply said, 'What sticks out for me is the faithfulness in prayer that we see in you and in your colleagues: the way you teach as well as practise that faithfulness, and help us all to build up the corporate life of prayer in the church. We've all learned to wait on God and his timing.'

As in the case of healing, this growing together in prayer has been a two-way matter. I have come down to the church six days a week for twelve years (days off being the exception) for morning prayer. Obviously such prayer times have varied in intensity and depth, but they have all been a focus for reading the Scriptures, praying for and joining in prayer with a wide range of people within the congregation and deanery. We prayed not only for the life and work of Aston, but also for the missionary work we are linked with worldwide.

Helga shares my vision of mission in the inner city. Together we've set aside a special hour of prayer each week for God's work to grow and develop as he desires. Helga's ministry has been one of encouragement and of helping to deepen the spiritual life of the parish. She was greatly involved in the Mothers' Union and started two home groups for housebound folk, which themselves became places where the prayer battle could go on. Working within the natural groupings in the church, then, we have as a church increased the armoury created by corporate prayer, and we have discovered a renewal of spiritual life and a strengthening for service in God's name. One thing led to another, for as we saw healings, our confidence grew in prayer, and we saw yet more miracles.

In 1980, for example, we had a parish mission which only took place after five years of steady prayer and preparation. Thus by the time Mission England meetings happened in 1984, we had grown sufficiently in prayer to pray confidently for people to come to new birth in Christ.

Another ministry that developed from our prayer life was DIAL—Dial Intercession and Love. At any time, anyone can ring a number and ask for prayer. A chain of prayer is set up so that within two hours as many as thirty people will be praying for the special need of the caller. In fact before I sat down to do this chapter (with every possible hurdle in my path—the move to Ulverston, burst pipes, and six bereavements in a week), Helga telephoned DIAL and asked for prayer that God would be glorified through the story I'm telling here.

All our work, then, starts on our knees, waiting on God.

Shoulder to shoulder

If ministry starts on our knees, it goes on as we walk and work together with our fellow Christians. My colleagues have contributed almost more than I can describe to our life there. Particularly at first (though also in latter years), when potential curates came to look at the parish, many went away and said they could not work in Aston. But those who did come blessed us deeply. First came Andy Gandon, from 1978–82. He was naturally gifted as a pastor and enormously deepened the pastoral ministry here. Growth in the inner city, as we discovered, has come much more through caring than through any other source.

My second colleague, Nick Ladd, lost his wife Sarah tragically in a car accident just weeks before he started his ministry here. He came burdened with grief and loneliness, and what a battle he fought! What a testimony to God's grace to local people in their own grief! But Nick was gifted as a Bible teacher, and as he emerged from the long tunnel of sorrow about two years after he arrived, he underwent a profound experience of renewal through attending a John Wimber conference. He poured himself then into caring for others, and he has become one of my closest friends.

Nick was followed in 1986 by Phil Evens, married to Pauline, with a grown up family. Phil is only a few years younger than I am, an experienced community and social worker with a great concern for justice in the inner city, and his arrival here is timely. As I go on to Ulverston, Phil remains behind to support my successor.

Phil in turn works closely with Martin and Suzette, the couple already mentioned, from CMS. From their flat in one of the high-rises, the Youngs provide advice, a local drop-in centre and caring for those around them. The network they have established in the local community points up clearly the value of relating the gospel to the needs of the inner city. The gulf has narrowed.

Does the left hand know what the right is doing?

Mission means starting with the people you find when you arrive in a new ministry. In Aston we found that at least a quarter of the congregation consisted of black Afro-Caribbeans. After about a year I discovered that the black Christians in our congregation didn't know each other; like most of the other whites in the congregation I had wrongly assumed at the outset that they were a group. Of course they weren't, any more than the whites. But neither were they in any position of leadership, nor contributing to any lay work in the church. It was important, therefore, to make sure that at the very least, the black families knew each other.

We started a meeting at the vicarage for twelve families. This soon developed into a Caribbean group that met monthly and invited other members of the congregation into its activities. Once blacks and whites were welded together in fellowship, the group as originally conceived died a natural death; it had fulfilled its intended function. We then worked positively, though without any fanfare, to make sure that both sides were fully involved in any new or re-evaluated parish activities: elections for the PCC, healing ministry, or evangelism—whatever it was. As a church we prayed and worked for full involvement on all sides.

Ten years on the lay ministry is fully integrated, and black members have felt free to express among us the deep hurt they felt on first arriving in England. Many had come as full members in the body of Christ and had looked forward to a warm reception from other Christians in this country. A few had indeed been welcomed, but many were not, and some were held deliberately at arm's length. White Christians can react in several ways to this: we can dismiss it, wallow in guilt, or we can simply confess it and move on in faith and fellowship together. As I leave Aston, I pray that God will lead this parish and others like it in inner cities across Britain to this kind of faith and fellowship together. In trust I look forward positively to the future.

Eyes to see the vision ahead

As one job after another—three in all—was offered to me, I realised the time was perhaps coming when Helga and I would have to leave Aston. At first there was no call or sign to move, just an expectation based on the three offers and the counsel of friends who felt that our ministry would not develop further if we stayed for ever in one place. Then in 1986 we had a mission to the congregation and all its contacts, and during the nurturing, training and preparation we saw a deepening of commitment for many lay leaders in the congregation. I realised that God was now calling us in a definite way to move on.

Early in 1987 I was invited to visit Ulverston. I confess that at first it didn't look right for us, but Helga and I fasted and prayed together to know the Lord's will. A prophecy had been given to us some months before, a verse which promised that God would do a 'new thing'. At the time, there seemed no particular application, but I had written down this prophecy as a reminder and had filed it among other church papers. Then, late one night while I was in prayer about Ulverston, the paper unexpectedly came to hand. This and many other factors confirmed our decision to move on.

The mission in Aston will go on. Phil Evens and I have a vision for a housing co-operative on an empty strip of land that adjoins church property. The church hopes to build as many as sixteen houses for singles, families, blacks and whites, and the elderly. Meanwhile, Martin Young, along with other lay people from the Aston and Handsworth forum of churches (formed after the violent riots in Handsworth and Lozelles two years ago), is hoping to be able to offer sound legal advice and to support many suffering severe deprivation in those areas.

For all the mission of Aston I pray that the work would continue to grow and be strengthened as a neighbourhood church ministering to the needs of others, witnessing to and winning those who have been traditionally estranged from the gospel of Jesus and from his church. Jesus died for them, though the church has not always shown them that he loves them where they are. Living out this love is what really matters.

Note

[1] CMS Newsletter, October 1985.

Chapter 8

St John's, Park, Sheffield

Graham Bewley

Graham Bewley has now left St John's, Park, and he writes much less of his own contribution to the church than of its contribution to him as a person and as a minister. He recounts lovingly the anguish of the Hyde Park flats, the noisy joyfulness of worship at St John's, the blossoming of people who meet Christ, and the hard lessons of street and pub. This chapter looks fearlessly at the face of the inner city—through the eyes of a man who knew himself to be an outsider but who through the love of God and of his local lay leaders became accepted as a member of the local Park community.

Now vicar of St Thomas in Kimberworth, Rotherham, Graham and his family still keep close links with Park through their daughter, Rachel, who remains there and feels it is her home. Graham describes himself as a passionate cyclist who bikes several thousand miles round his parish every year. He and his Canadian wife Gill have two other children, Claire and Andrew.

Success or failure

Right at the beginning let us recall some poignant words by the great Japanese Christian Toyohiko Kagawa: 'There are two kinds of Christianity: success Christianity and failure Christianity.'[1] We do well to ponder this before I tell the story of what might be described as the beginning of one 'successful' church in the inner city—St John's, Park, Sheffield. What follows is inevitably impressionistic; it is what I recall as vicar of St John's for some seven and a half years. I trust I have not been too selective, for the story remains a valid testimony to what God did during those years: for me, for other members of staff and—most importantly of all—for the continuing members of St John's congregation.

'What have you done wrong to get Park?' was a fellow-clergyman's response to my telling him I was about to start a new ministry in the inner city. And that tone conveying 'grot!' was not just the reaction to our own move into the 'living' of Park; it is true of anyone else moving into Park. The fairly typical reaction is that most want to leave as fast as they arrive. Hyde Park flats in particular are a 'community in transit'; when most people sign to take possession of a flat they also sign a housing transfer form.

Not that the flats were always this way. When they were put up in the early 1960s—flats to house 3,500 people—they were seen as a great breakthrough in housing the working class. And (to be fair to architects, planners and builders) they were replacing some shocking slum back-to-back property. Twenty-five years on, they are no longer seen as an award-winning housing complex; rather, they are seen by the majority of both those who live there and local officials as what the local newspaper calls 'a lament'. Some of the National Census figures for 1981 speak for themselves: city population 12,138; adult unemployment 25 per cent (31 per cent male); unemployment of sixteen to nineteen-year-olds 34 per cent; council housing 93 per cent; household with no car 80 per cent; degree and professional qualifications 2 per cent; single-parent households 10 per cent.

When we arrived in the parish eight years ago, we came with the assumption that it *was* possible for this to be a living community. Today such optimism has become tarnished, and the vision has faded. Like so many other vast blocks of flats, Hyde Park would be better destroyed. Over the years the community has constantly deteriorated, with resultant anger among many who have lived through the decline: 'We didn't want to leave, it's central to town, near the markets, and the flats are warm—there are so many good things about the flats. But things got worse and worse: noise, dog muck, rubbish—we've just got to get off.' (We shall return to some of the 'good things', but most would move if they could.)

Wybourn

Another very important part of St John's parish is the large Wybourn estate, pre-war but recently modernised. Though as in many other areas of our inner cities much needs to be done, Wybourn is in comparison with the Hyde Park and Park Hill flats a much more settled community. There is some movement ('flitting') on the estate but most people want to stay; they are usually only looking for more appropriate accommodation as their families increase.

St John's Church

Built in 1838, it has remained over the years firmly within the evangelical tradition of the Church of England. Even its architecture depicts a 'preaching church'. This emphasis has continued following a major reappointing of its interior in the 1970s. Now all the furniture is movable—table, pulpit, prayer desks, pews, etc; this mobility also lends enormous flexibility to worship, drama groups, concerts or whatever activity takes place. Discussion is still going on as to the possible use of the nave as a badminton court—the argument being it is morally wrong to maintain a building simply for a few hours' worship each week. Other activities are also being considered.

All this reuse of the church building has one more vital element to it; it is the outreach of the church to the community. Most working-class people (men in particular) find it very difficult even to enter a church—'What will me mates say?'—so if the church is used other than for worship, a further bridge is built.

The previous incumbent made two extremely significant moves during his ministry. He first sought to make St John's a church of the immediate parish. This meant that many who came in from outside the parish were asked to consider attending their own local church—a bold step for it meant real decline in membership and income, but a very necessary step for the future local growth to happen. He also established a shared leadership team in order to share his responsibilities with four lay leaders (three men and one woman) in addition to the assistant staff. They met fortnightly to pray, discuss and plan together.

It must be emphasised that much of the later growth at St John's would not have happened if these two courageous steps had not been taken previously. Thus when I was appointed the incumbent of St John's there was already a small, prayerful nucleus of people looking for growth and expansion.

'Dream dreams and see visions'

A number of years ago Bishop Michael Whinney, then vicar of St James, Bermondsey, shared his dream with others in an article in *Christians in Industrial Areas*.[2] His dream became ours; because it was so significant, I'll report it in full:

Let me tell you about it ... it was Sunday morning and the Christians were arriving at their meeting-place. They came from all directions, in ones and twos, families and groups of friends and neighbours. Some cars bringing elderly and handicapped people drove up to the door, and helping hands were there to guide or push or carry. By 11 o'clock the place was happily chatty and fairly full, and the ministers and elders led the first part of the worship.

Hymns and choruses, prayers and Bible reading had their place in the pattern—it was a fairly regular pattern, especially to help the children join in and follow more easily. About a dozen (both children and adults) had brought their musical instruments and played during some of the singing. People had handed in their special requests for prayer on arrival, and the person leading the prayers prayed accordingly.

Then after half an hour or so groups of the different ages disappeared into smaller rooms leading off the main worship area, while most of the adults gathered together at the front; this was the half-hour period for the ministry of the word. One group was having discussion based on a Bible passage; one of the younger groups was busy cutting out, painting and putting together figures about a Bible story; another group was acting a modern version of the Good Samaritan; yet another was listening to a serious talk about the Bible teaching on life after death. Sometimes these groups were not split according to age; on some Sundays whole families would go off to a room together, and the mums and dads would work with and help their children, a popular event because it didn't happen too often!

Soon after 12 noon, everyone was back in the main area again; people sang for a while, waiting for the later returners (those who just couldn't leave their painting and sticking!). Quietness descended as the bread and wine were put on the central table, and the Lord's Supper—the Holy Communion—began. In the well-remembered words about Jesus breaking bread and saying, 'This is my body which was broken for you...Do this in remembrance of me', we thought of the cross and the mighty resurrection that followed. Quietly in groups people came out and stood or knelt round the table in a big circle, some children with their parents, others with 'adopted parents' for the occasion. Then the bread and wine were taken. Next another group came forward, shared and returned; then another and another until all had been united before the Lord. The occasional child's cry worried no one as they were a family together, and that was just part of life. With a prayer as they offered themselves to God to take charge of them, strengthen them and go with them into the world he had made, and with a final hymn saying 'thank you' to the great Lord Jesus, the worship ended.

But people didn't go home—no, everyone moved into the nearby large room (used by the various age groups for mid-week evening activities and a daytime play group and lunch club) and the food that practically everyone had brought in containers was unpacked. Family tables included those who were on their own, and everyone sat with someone else. People moved from table to table chatting and helping. There was even a nineteen-year-old university student, a boy helping a mother with four young children, giving the baby its bottle!

At about 1.15 or 1.30 pm, when the children had roamed around and were getting a bit restless, guitars were twanged and people called out their choice of hymns and choruses. A group of young adults sang a moving Negro spiritual. A youth leader invited any interested children to join him for some games in the play area outside. This helped others to relax and join in the time of exchanging news that followed. News was told of how God had helped in many ordinary everyday practical ways during the week; many were clear answers to last week's prayers, and so many offered prayers of 'thank you God'. Then came the problems and sorrows and prayer requests for others in need. People prayed aloud from where they sat at the tables and others joined in their prayers in their hearts. Laughter and tears came and went; the concern was to do with real life as it is day by day.

By 2.30 things were more or less over. Those at a loose end were planning the afternoon; some were going off to visit those alone in hospital; others were going off as families to see relatives; another party was going to Epping Forest for an outing. Those who wanted a quiet snooze were welcome to stay in one of the rest rooms in the building. The Christian family split up and went its separate ways.

They didn't have another service that night; instead, families met together for tea and in the evening, just enjoying being together. Single people who wanted to come out again met in friends' flats nearby. People always knew who was holding 'open house' that night, and often they met in the home of a senior citizen who couldn't get out. This sort of company was like heaven to that lonely person!

I felt the day had been a little bit of heaven on earth. Need it remain just a dream?

Pioneering

And so we made a start. We saw ourselves as pioneers; thus, trying to impart traditional (and for the most part meaningless) Anglicanism was ruled out as a non-starter. *Faith in the City* states, 'Our evidence suggests that it is the consistently middle-class presentation of the gospel and style of church life which create a gulf between it and most working-class people.'[3] This dilemma we had to acknowledge before God and before the church at large, often to the annoyance of fellow-clergy and their congregations. Some of them saw St John's as the rebellious church, which increasingly 'did its own thing'. Always to be on the receiving end of such criticism is painful; it was easy to become a martyr!

Although Mike Whinney's 'dream' played a vital part in our growth at St John's, I was far more committed to forming groups of those genuinely looking for faith who in their own homes could share their questions and doubts about Christian faith. Logically working through a series of questions about God, they would supposedly come to place their faith in Jesus Christ. Such a process never got off the ground! Perhaps it would work at university and in some middle-class parishes, but not among working-class men and women. Christian faith for most working-class people is initially 'caught' not 'taught'. The gospel must become visible. (See 1 Jn 1:1,2, and Jesus' words to the enquiring Andrew, '"Come and *see*"...so they went with him and *saw*...and spent the rest of that day with him' Jn 1:39.) And so in working to embody the gospel we felt we were pioneering in this working-class area.

Worship Radio 2-style

When we drew up 'Purposes, Aims and Objectives' for the parish, worship came at the head of the list. Eddie Neale's stimulating article 'Worship' was circulated to the lay leaders, and lively discussions ensued.[4] We felt that most traditional worship—be it Anglican, Free Church or even Roman—is quite simply boring. Most of the problem is the *music*. Classical music may be an expression of joy to the initiated, but for most working-class people it is a dirge. We need a music that expresses joy in the culture of the people! This meant that Radio 2, not Radio 3, was our norm. First a single guitar led our music spot; later, other instruments joined and we began to clap. Choruses became a new litany and from them most people learned their theology, as many Christians from former centuries have learned their theology from the Prayer Book! As we improved and relaxed, the singing led by the music group reduced many folk to tears; it was the high point of the service, though uncomfortable for a traditional Anglican.

To most working-class people silence is either boring or threatening. (I never ask to have the TV turned off when visiting—down possibly, but *never* off! To be left alone with the vicar is bad enough, but without the telly ridiculous.) This is not to say that silence can never be a part of worship, the timing must be right. Again, before and after worship a record was played, sometimes Jim Reeves, sometimes Fisherfolk. The church building has become a place to feel at home in. In such an atmosphere people could chatter and even shout at each other, 'Ay up, all right Fred?' Occasionally the record player didn't work or was forgotten and the resulting atmosphere was cold. It is generally true that working-class people worship in noise—happy, relaxed, joyous noise!

Matthew Dieppe, drawing upon the research of Bernstein on the use of language by the working class says, 'It is a language lacking in adjectives and adverbs, lacking in variety...often less effective in conveying information than gestures and attitudes which carry particular meanings.'[5] Feelings, then, are rarely verbalised. Touch, sight, hearing, even smell play a vital part in conveying the message. And yet most traditional worship is one mass of words from start to finish. This is not to say that words aren't important, but we have to watch the way we use them and use them sparingly. *Faith in the City* comments, 'To give people a 1,300-page Alternative Service Book is a symptom of the gulf between church and ordinary people in the UPA'.[6] Indeed, the report states that reforming the liturgy has really only just begun for the UPA church!

This is possibly the place to mention the fact that following our experiences at St John's we would wish to qualify the maxim 'Working-class people don't read.' In fact once the motivation to read is there, these folk see the Bible as God's primary means of declaring his truth to us, and read they will! Often the reading does not begin alone but with others, discussing the word together. Once the preacher had expounded a passage he or she was frequently told at the door, 'I must go and read that again later on.' Incidentally, my wife sold over sixty *Good News* Bibles over the years we were at St John's.

We made two more relevant discoveries about language. The use of the royal 'we' demands a sophistication not usually found among the average congregation—even the Taizé office has dropped it! Working-class people are generally immediate in their appreciation or rejection. As we began to produce our own forms of worship, the personal pronoun became more and more important. This we found particularly important in the confession. People came with real needs, and somehow they had to express their own feelings and speak about their own sins. To say, 'We have left undone those things we ought to have done, and have done those things we ought not to have done' is far too vague and remote. Prayer—confession in particular—needs to be concrete. Bad temper and angry words—these are real emotions, real sins experienced during the week; they need to be expressed specifically to God and to others.

We discovered, too, that some of the words of the charismatic choruses are inappropriate. How a South Yorkshire miner or ex-steel worker can sing, 'Jesus, how lovely you are' is quite frankly beyond the imagination. But he will sing till he bursts, 'Jesus you're terrific, I really think you are, You took me from the dustbin, and you treat me like a star.'

I realise that even the hardest of men and women have a soft spot somewhere, but we must not present a weak, soft Jesus. (Consider the 'manly' Christianity of—say—*Chariots of Fire*.) What I mean is that working-class people are (and have to be) quite physical, and somehow their experience of life must be reflected in the Jesus they experience.

Ministry of the word

In the revamping of our morning worship we felt that following a lectionary or church's year wouldn't be very helpful. We needed to go back to basics. Our theology would grow up from our needs, our situation, not something imposed from the top down and furthermore which assumed far too much background knowledge. So we decided to work our way through Luke's Gospel. Copies of the *Good News* Luke's Gospel were purchased and provided for each member of the congregation. Whoever read the lesson introduced it something like this: 'Morning everybody! Now today's reading is taken from Luke chapter — verses — and you find that on page — right, got it? This tells us about…' It is then the task of the preacher to expound and proclaim and make the passage live. The use of an overhead projector, questions to the congregation, questions or comments *from* the congregation and for the preacher. 'A congregation' it is said, 'preaches half the sermon.' Without a doubt that is the experience at St John's. Sometimes it gets a bit unruly (and why not?) but generally the rapport between preacher and congregation is infinitely better than when the preacher stands six feet above contradiction. As the years went by, complete Bibles replaced the somewhat dog-eared Gospels.

Our meeting with God and with one another in worship needs the element of entertainment about it all, often brought in by the person leading the worship or preaching. Again, this means there can't be any sameness about it; if there is to be 'clockwork worship', why not put on a tape recorder? We developed a series of services on various coloured pages, and no one knew what service was coming until the actual service began. Increasingly, laypeople were leading the worship, and each brought his or her own distinctive personality to bear upon the worship—a kaleidoscope of emerging talents and gifts. Not that the transformation of our morning worship thrilled everyone. Some just didn't take to such radical changes. Some left, some very hurt; other 'oldies' were either big enough or confident enough to see *why* the change was necessary. 'I don't like the change myself' said one person to me, 'but I see God at work'—we embraced each other. 'We're a family and it's good to be together.'

'I know I am loved'

Under God our family worship became a place where Christians were built up in their faith and where new people could come without feeling awkward. There was an easy unchurchy atmosphere; people could relax, 'Ay it's really friendly, isn't it?' said a somewhat astonished newcomer. So new people were integrated into the congregation, and not just by the clergy on duty but by the congregation themselves.

The following poem written by someone right outside the life of the church will witness to this reality—we don't get poems like this every week, though!

Fighting My Way Back

I'm rebuilding my faith in Jesus,
Nothing is going to shake it,
With the love of Christians around me,
I know I am going to make it.
It's going to be a hard climb,
Meeting obstacles all the way,
To me it may seem a long time,
But it will happen one day.
I was given the courage I needed,
By the word of a very dear friend,
At the time she couldn't have known
Just where it all would end.
With a pounding heart I entered the church,
Not knowing what I would find—
An outstretched hand bid me welcome,
I have never known folk so kind...
People I've never known,
Took my hand, to show me they cared,
Saying, troubles are often easier,

When with the Lord they're shared.
Graham is working with me,
To show me the way back to God's love,
Give me peace in my heart on earth,
Prepare me for heaven above.

The privilege of ministry in such an atmosphere is beyond words!

Evangelism wasn't something put on as an event—it just happened week by week. There was no pressure of logically working out questions set by others to newcomers. Instead, here they were loved, accepted, received—'grasped by love' is what the gospel is all about. And so when the local newspaper asked why people go to church (after the Bishop of Sheffield said he wanted Anglicans to find ways of boosting church attendance), we simply passed round pencils and papers. We asked the congregation to jot down the reason they came to church. Their answers spoke of their experiences of love:

'To worship Jesus who is a Saviour and friend'
'To be with God'
'To worship God and meet my Christian mates'
'I go to church for peace and love that God gives me'.

Housegroups—looking after each other outside Sunday

Our next priority was the building up of the Christian community outside Sunday. We also needed to bring newcomers to a place of trust and commitment to Jesus Christ, and this meant the forming of house groups in various parts of the parish.

We wrestled with the question of making them either local or self-selecting, and in the end opted for making them locally based. This would enable people to get together with each other outside the fortnightly house group meeting and encourage a concern for each particular area, and for the individuals and families who lived nearby.

(How far we ever really achieved the latter aim I doubt; maybe folk were not yet confident enough.)

That first group

We can well remember how in our first house group on the Wybourn estate we played 'Pit' together for weeks, thanks to a suggestion by David Sheppard from his Mayflower days. Bridges were built; we laughed together and gradually opened ourselves to each other. Slowly we brought in the explicitly spiritual dimension with prayer and then Bible study. I can remember walking back to the vicarage with my wife, saying, 'I wonder if we're getting anywhere?' She knew we were—Gill's better at waiting, maybe from years of shopping!

The real breakthrough came when we took one of J B Phillips' plays from his *A Man Called Jesus*. We had struggled with straight Bible study, using various creative methods but once we had some action, other senses were evoked. Then dormant members came to life. Peter was suddenly a real person, as were the other disciples and Jesus. Phillips' words were thrown out as we provided our own—'No, I think Peter said it this way.' After several rehearsals we performed the play at the family worship.

Be fruitful and multiply

During the time Gill and I were forming our first house group, other Christians were busy forming other groups. 'Lord,' prayed one of our lay leaders one night, 'there are many hurt people in our church.' And so the house groups have become places of love and support for each other. Not that it was all 'sweetness and light'! Wherever various temperaments and personalities meet together there are inevitable frictions and tensions. Do we behave in an immature way and run away from conflict, or under God's Spirit and prayer do we seek to make them creative? All growth is painful—especially in the body of Christ. Again such pain can be caused when a group which has grown too large has to split into two smaller groups.

Maintaining the various groups was never easy—they would inevitably rise and fall, but there is no question that without such groups St John's would never have survived; they were the backbone to all we did. Like Abbé Godin before us in *France Pagan?* we found that 'it is in clusters that they will cling to Christ, the living vine'.[8]

We were anxious that the groups should not be just spiritual hot-houses, cliques of like-minded members, so we encouraged them to have a varied programme: meals out together (watching the cost because of unemployment), a drink at the local pub, a social evening, a weekend away together. Each group had its own leader and chose its own programme. Again each group had a full range of ages—we had closed down all other separate sex age groups, though not with the happiest results.

The day-to-day pastoral care by members of house groups was at times very moving indeed. We can recall an older woman who had come to faith following the death of her husband. She would meet regularly with a new family to read and pray together several times a week. They encouraged each other—building up each other in their new faith. Without such human contact they would have remained isolated and alone.

As I think about it now, we didn't take enough pastoral care of the house group leaders themselves, especially in the early days. It was a bit of a 'sink or swim' policy. Somehow we managed, and a bi-monthly leaders' meeting was established. Towards the end of our time at St John's a lass with great group management skills ran a series of sessions on such topics as handling conflict creatively, maintaining interest, helping individuals.

Welcome group

Running parallel with the house groups was another group we called the 'Welcome Group'. This was a group for new-comers who were wanting to explore what it meant to be a Christian. Like a house group it met fortnightly but had a more planned programme, though time was given to mem-bers to allow them to raise their own particular interests and concerns. At the end of a year there was the option of confirmation—a high point for many people. We spent this long time together as a group for we felt this enabled people to settle and to open up to each other. Usually once a per-son had finished Welcome Group they joined a regular house group, though sometimes folk were in both groups concurrently.

Material is never easy to choose, but in the end we found the 'Question Mark' booklets published by Scripture Union the most useful: an evocative picture, a limited number of words and a stimulating question. Over and over again it was remarked how this teaching was like that of Jesus. We since have been thrilled with some of the material from the Evangelical Urban Training Project.[9]

Hang in there baby!

An illustration of how far most churches are removed from a great number of people is shown by the following conver-sation. After a couple of sessions in the Welcome Group one lad came up and said to me, 'I don't think I'm coming any more.'

'Why not?' I retorted, grieved and hurt— it had taken a lot of hard work to get him even to one session.

'Well, when I was at school,' he continued, 'I got all the questions wrong. You see I'm not very good on things like that. When I came here, what did we do? More questions. And I'll only get them all wrong again, so what's the point!'

I tried to persuade him to think again but I already knew he would never return.

Groups are vital for most folk—or least a great number. But when the material is presented in a package, often wrapped up in an alien culture, of course it is rejected. Maybe for people like Fred the vital ingredient is personal contact—hours of friendship, going to the pub, watching football, just being a mate. Commitment to Jesus Christ will come unexpectedly, at the end of a long and often costly road, involving many bridges. Maybe I need to sit at the feet of overseas missionaries who have worked in North Africa; Max Warren talked about 'long-term loving'.

Flowering and blossoming

What began to emerge from our Christian worship on Sundays and from the fellowship of the house groups was above all a new sense of worth by individuals. They received a new identity, a new self-image. And that is the good news of Jesus—to be 'grasped by love'. When that happens—and it is a privilege beyond all comparison both to observe and to be involved in—people begin to flower, blossom: the bud which has been shut for so long begins to open in the warmth of love and acceptance. We begin to see great beauty in people.

The healing of hurt people (and that means most of us) must always have a part of the total programme of ministry in any local church if it is to share in the compassion of Christ. The pitfalls and heartaches of such a ministry are legion, particularly so when much of the local culture is based on immediate gratification.

St John's has faced struggles over the healing ministry, which usually takes place once a month in the evening worship. Possibly the most effective form of healing is the loving touch of another in the name of the Lord Jesus.

Here I must mention the healing group, established mainly through the vision and persistence of Pippa Winton, our deacon. A sizeable number in the congregation would have liked more frequent and explicit use of various forms of healing. To be honest, I was—and remain so—more cautious. But it is only natural that in any growing church there are areas of conflict, and for us healing was one.

Two other areas of strategy are important: firstly, we had a fairly 'firm' baptismal policy (ie church attendance plus several periods of instruction, plus the use of a Thanksgiving and Blessing as a pastoral alternative). This stance has borne fruit in that various people who came to baptism preparation now hold vital positions in the life of St John's. Secondly, we made a special effort to reach families, aware at the same time of the need to be sensitive to the great numbers of single parents, single people, and elderly in the parish. As the 1977 National Evangelical Congress at Keele concluded, and as we have discovered, 'We assert our faith that God is able to create and maintain local leadership in any community!'

This new confidence, new self-worth, meant we were able to move on in our understanding of leadership in the local church. Though we had never had a pyramid model of leadership because of our regular meeting of lay leaders and staff, we felt it was right to take into our system local elders. This development wasn't hurried, and after weeks of discussion and prayer, plans culminated in a weekend away for the PCC and the staff. What emerged was that the elders, with the other staff, would lead the spiritual aspect of the church's ministry, leaving administration, finance and fabric in the hands of the PCC. This compartmentalising of work has never proved easy; there is much overlapping, but at least it provided a general structure within which everyone's gifts could contribute to the whole.

Muckers

Another area of growing confidence and self-worth was the presentation of the gospel musical 'Muckers'. It all began one day as I was walking our dog. A local publican called me across. 'You know, Graham, I see thee as one of me muckers.'

'What on earth's a mucker?'

'A mucker is me friend, mate, buddy.'

A nice moment. Isn't it good to be human—and I didn't even regularly drink in his pub.

This story caught the imagination of one of our members when I related it to the congregation. Before long a play was written set in the 1920s on the Wybourn estate. Poor, rough, tough—but full of cameraderie, with mum boss in the house, eldest lad leader of the gang outside. Jesus comes to the Wybourn! One by one the family are converted and finally Bill comes saying to the Lord, 'From now on thee and me are muckers.'

It was a totally local performance. On the first night I sat in St John's nave, now being used as a theatre, open-mouthed at the talent, joy, growth and confidence which emerged—unbelievable! Here was a further flowering, blossoming of individuals and a group under the Spirit of God. And possibly the most important ingredient was that it was *their* play, *their* musical, authentic Wybourn. It ran for several nights and later to the entire deanery. Here was incarnational theology at its best—'Yer don't have to be posh to love Jesus.' And to see steel workers, miners wet-eyed and engrossed, demonstrates how effective local drama can be.

Our church holidays also played an important part of building up the body of Christ, deepening relationships and widening people's visions of something more than Skeggy. For many it was a first Christian holiday. At times it was sheer delight to see people enjoying each other. I must give credit to the fact that most of the

holiday was lay-led—a further example of lay initiative and
vision.

Ministry—a partnership

We have learnt over the years the vitally important concept
in ministry of both local and 'imported' leadership. The
local person is trained on the job, so is less likely to lose
contact with local people; he or she has grown up among
them. Again they act as a filter through which what we
sought to communicate to others could pass. 'That'll never
work here' was their response to so much of the official
church's literature and programmes. *Faith in the City* says
much the same thing: 'For the most part Christian theology
has been created by those relatively well provided with
leisure, freedom of action and material well being.' Again,
'Our evidence suggests that it is the consistently middle-
class presentation of the gospel and style of church life
which creates a gulf between it and most working-class
people.' The result must be that the church must 'attend to
the voices, the experience, and the spiritual riches of the
poor in its midst'.[10]

'Imported' staff members have much to offer to this
partnership as well. They usually come with new ideas, a
greater vision and depth to the ministry and the life of the
church. It is very easy for a local church to become pre-
occupied with itself—this is even more of a temptation in
the inner city where people, through no fault of their own,
have limited horizons. Staff can support and encourage
local elders in their exercise of ministry of authority. We
must stand together as team—not always easy!

Elders—a case of learning lessons

The appointment of elders we achieved on the principle of

mutual recognition of gifts of leadership and spirituality. The initial candidates were selected by the staff but with the full support of the PCC and congregation. Further elders will be selected by staff and the present elders, but again fully recognised by the congregation. But I wish we had involved the bishop in the actual commissioning of the elders. This would have helped get over the problem of St John's feeling 'We can do it our way.' (To some degree this was understandable; when you've been on the receiving end for most of your life, and that's the way society works, but then you begin to hold your head high and 'walk tall', you want to crow a bit!) But St John's is not an independent Free Church; it is part of the wider Anglican Communion and needs for its own life and for the life of the Anglican Communion to learn to relate to it. Again it is a question of partnership, the local church maintaining and developing its own life but not to the exclusion of the wider church. We need each other, to learn and to receive from one another. This is important; historically, most independent churches have left the inner city.

There was also the knotty problem of women becoming elders. Frankly, we were divided and remain so. Of course, there is a security for some who read the Bible literally on the subject—no hermeneutical problem for them! Yet alongside this approach is another seeing women as gifted by God and needing to exercise their gifts of ministry.

Moving out—*shalom*

Much of our effort over the years has been to establish a Christian community true and authentic for our local culture: 'to give every encouragement to the growth of theologies that are authentic expressions of local cultures'.[11] From this base, to which we could return again and again, we could move out into the wider community. Again we would want to echo the findings of *Faith in the City*. 'The

evidence of the Gospels makes it clear that Jesus' procla-
mation of the kingdom of God had from the start profound
social and political implications.'[12] As people's self-image
and worth began to develop, so their confidence to move
out and make their contribution to the enormous problems
facing the inner city began to be realised.

The contribution that St John's has made to the wider
community has been considerable. I wish I had room to pay
tribute to it all! Tenants' associations, school governing
bodies, local Labour party, mental health, mother and
toddler groups—these are but a few of the ways members
have been involved in practical caring. But once involved
one soon realises that in fighting for rights (among many
was concern about racism, rates, and the CND) one is
fighting against principalities and powers in high places.
Evil is indeed (as Marx once pointed out) 'not just in the
human heart but in the very structures of economic and
social relationships'.[13] Still, this network of membership
involvement has enabled St John's to have a voice in the
community and among the many secular workers in the
area.

God outside the church

Our involvement in the wider community has taught us
many things. The first is that God is concerned with issues
that aren't simply spiritual. The Hebrew word *shalom* came
to mean a great deal to us. Politics, community affairs,
housing, education, (un)employment, health were not to
be seen as an extra to our agenda. Indeed the physical and
corporate belongs together with the spiritual as part of salvation. The following two quotations will, I hope, help to
make this clear. '*Shalom* means total harmony within the
community. It is founded upon order and permeated by
God's blessing and hence makes it possible for men to develop and increase, free and unhindered on every side.'[14]

My own favourite definition of *shalom* comes from Bishop John Taylor: '*Shalom*', he says, 'is something much broader than "peace": *the harmony of a caring community informed at every point by its awareness of God*' [emphasis mine]. And in that definition the kernel of *shalom*'s meaning is in the phrase "at every point". It speaks of a wholeness that is complete because every aspect and every corner of ordinary life is included.[15]

The practical working out of that God-given vision of *shalom* in our community took every ounce of effort we could possess. We had to return again and again to prayer that God would direct our efforts in bringing *shalom* to our community.

I began this chapter with a lack of optimism about the quality of life now expected in the Hyde Park flats. That, I'm afraid, must still remain the overwhelming impression. Nevertheless, over the years many good things have happened. One of the lasting signs of *shalom* has been the replacement of the local dog track with a recreation ground. Gone are the kennels, the smell, the massive rats and barking dogs. Instead have come trees, swings, grass, a football pitch, the laughter of happy families playing. Everyday kindnesses grow in Hyde Park. A single lass moved in to the flats. She told me, 'Twelve people from Hyde Park were there helping me scrub floors and walls, carrying boxes and furniture.' Again, £900 was raised towards the Sheffield Hospital body scanner. And one of the most impressive areas of caring (and that right outside the church) was that a number of social workers and residents were becoming increasingly concerned over the number of ex-patients from the local mental health hospital (Middlewood) being dumped at Hyde Park flats. A mental health group was formed; hours of work were put in to establish the facts—actual numbers, amount of after-care, length of stay. The result was a dramatic drop in the number of ex-patients being dumped, plus a much greater care for those who did stay. Another sign of *shalom*.

'My body shall set mankind free '

Such signs of *shalom* outside church forces the church to be the sign of the kingdom within the community. The concluding section will try to focus on a few aspects of being this sign to others.

Scaffolding and partnership

As George Burton before us, we said in our early days, 'Until local people are ready to take over the running of things, outside help will be needed to get the work started. It is important that people who do come from a different background to work in an area like ours should not let their behaviour be governed simply by their upbringing or by the pattern or code of life that they have received!' He adds, 'I do not believe that middle-class culture and way of life is any better than that of the working-class.' So, coming in from outside we must 'try to distinguish between what is morally wrong and what is socially wrong or unconventional'.[16] That is not easy but is absolutely essential.

The mixing of backgrounds can bring real tension, but that tension needs to be creative, a learning from each other. There shouldn't be too many outsiders who want to take over everything! A further qualification of those wanting to act as 'scaffolding' is either that they live in the area, or if that is not possible, then as near to the parish as possible. At St John's it was simply delicious to see Christians from vastly different backgrounds loving and sharing with each other. ('See how these Christians love one another!') And this has done much in our evangelism—the gospel became visible before it became audible.

This meant that we were not quite so happy with the word 'scaffolding'. Scaffolding implies once the structure has been built, the scaffolding is taken away. It is not easy to maintain oneness, for those who come from more confident backgrounds easily slip into their naturally assertive roles, especially in crises. But we do search for partnership with each other, focusing on oneness in Christ; and we struggle to be a creative example to the rest of the community.

Bridges

Christians are called to be bridge people, to be stepping stones whereby non-Christians move closer to their commitment to Christ and his kingdom, and to their final integration into the body of Christ. Bridge building is a key part of the work of partnership.

The pub Here is the natural place where a great number of working-class people relax, and friendships are formed. It is an important feature of working-class culture and so must be taken seriously. For most people pub and church don't mix. On either side, the feeling is often mutual. If a regular at the pub started coming to church his entrance fee would be to stop going to the local boozer. So if local Christians can regularly attend a local pub, an enormous number of barriers are broken down, even more so if the group of Christians are seen to be actually enjoying themselves. Absolute amazement if the vicar is among them!!

Group/herd mentality I once met a friend from the Wybourn estate who told me he was leaving. 'Leaving the Wybourn?' I asked with astonishment.

'Oh, I'm only flitting house. I was born here, and I'll die here.'

Here on the Wybourn he belonged; this was his group. If ever that person and his cronies are to be won for Christ, we must win not just him as an individual, but the whole group.

The same is true of winning men and women in pub culture. To ask or expect an individual from a group of drinking friends to enter a church on his own is like asking for the moon. Solidarity is a dominant feature of working-class culture, and individualism conditions the working class against even hearing the gospel. Where group loyalty is strong then the only hope is to win the group as a whole. We have made little progress in such group evangelism, though it is obviously an integral feature of outreach in the New Testament and on the overseas mission field. Abbé Michonneau would go so far as to say:

> They think as a unit and subscribe only to those ideas which the group holds...it is impossible to draw them to Christ as individuals. Either the whole group goes over to him, or no one does. The conquest must be a collective one. That does not mean a conquest of the entire working class but this group, or this portion here and now.[17]

And so Mission Sheffield made little impact on us, either in the outreach itself and even less so in the follow-up.

Football team Much of working-class culture is physical, so football is very much a part of that physical culture. St John's football team plays a very important role in outreach to men. To see men and lads known as Christians in the area playing hard on the football field is an important bridge for many outsiders. Friendships are established, and on neutral territory, both on the field and in the pub afterwards.

The place of the vicar Some would say, 'The clergyman as such must go, if the locals are to be the evangelists of the area.' After several years in the inner city I believe this is far too facile a comment. We're back to partnership again. Innumerable doors were opened to the vicar of the parish as an evangelist—but in this role I had to earn the right. I well remember my first entry into a rough pub in the area. The moment I walked through the door cat calls and cigarette packets were thrown. I moved across to the bar.

'What do you want?' the landlord asked curtly.

'I don't want fish and chips! A pint of bitter please.'

'Never 'ad a vicar in this pub before.'

'You've got him now!' No one spoke to me—I downed my pint and left, having thought I had been to purgatory! But the next time I entered the same pub my pint was bought for me—'We were just testing you out.' I have had more worthwhile conversations in that pub than in any other in the parish.

Working-class people are still very traditional at heart; they don't want to discard the vicar, for they would feel deserted. But the old idea of being the driver and conductor of the bus while everyone else is a passenger must go once and for all. Yet that isn't easy: I vividly recall when sitting in the congregation on a Sunday evening, having done nothing 'up front' all day, I said to myself, 'What on earth have I been ordained for?' One of the most salutary but uncomfortable answers I had came when I was talking to one of our Christian leaders and saying something like, 'You know, our coming to live in Park has been one of the most enriching experiences of our lives.'

'It may be enriching for you at the top, but I'm not sure what it has meant to us at the bottom.' And the man just looked right at me.

It took me about a week to get over that remark, and I don't think I'm quite over it now. But it does reveal the hurt felt by many in the inner city if there is even the suggestion of a patronising ministry.

Courage Christians who dare to live on estates are brave indeed. The sheltered atmosphere of suburbia knows nothing of the hassle and cost that living as a Christian (family) can bring. I can well recall seeing a lad from the estate shaking before entering the pub to sing carols at Christmas, 'Ay up, Graham, I used to drink with me mates in this pub.' It took guts to sing in front of them. I remember the warmth, love, honesty and generosity of fellow Christian human beings as we met on the street or in church Sunday by Sunday. 'And like their Latin American brothers and sisters they will thus cease to be consumers of spiritualities that are doubtless valid but that nonetheless reflect other experiences and other goals for they are *carrying out their own way of being faithful* both to the Lord and to the experiences of the poorest.'[18]

We are the product of our environment, and so often that deadens people, 'people who don't believe in themselves, prisoners of incurable timidity, those who have no imagination by which to plan a better future and no personality with which to achieve it. They are the poorest...They are the silent ones who live without touching anything, or even wanting to.'[19] But to them Jesus said, 'Yours is the kingdom of heaven.' *Shalom.*

Notes

[1] Toyohiko Kagawa, *Meditations on the Cross* (SCM Press: London, 1936), p 21.

[2] Michael Whinney, article in *Christians in Industrial Areas* (CIIA), no 26 (edited slightly). Throughout this essay I shall be drawing up various articles which have appeared in that now defunct magazine. I wish to pay tribute to it as being seminal in so much of our thinking. *The City Cries* is the CIIA's latest journal.

[3] *Faith in the City* (Church House Publishing: London, 1985), p 66.

[4] *CIIA* no 10.

[5] *CIIA* no 5.

[6] *Faith in the City*, *op cit*, p 136.

[7] David Kibble, 'The Protestant Liturgy and the Working Classes', *Liturgical Review*, vol VII (1976). He develops many of the themes here only touched upon; it is worth consulting.

[8] Maisie Ward, *France Pagan?* (The Mission of Abbé Godin: Sheed and Ward), p 147.

[9] I should also mention their excellent pastoral care course—details from them.

[10] *Faith in the City*, *op cit*, pp 62–66.

[11] *ibid*, p 65.

[12] *ibid*, p 48.

[13] *ibid*, p 51.

[14] Heinrich Gross in *Encyclopedia of Biblical Theology*.

[15] John Taylor, *Enough is Enough* (Hodder and Stoughton: 1975), p 41.

[16] George Burton, *People Matter More Than Things* (Hodder and Stoughton: 1965), pp 32–36.

[17] Abbé Michonneau, *Mission in Industrial France* (now out of print).

[18] Gustavo Gutierrez, *We Drink from Our Own Wells* (SCM Press: London, 1984).

[19] Luigi Santucci, *Wrestling With Christ* (Collins:1969), p 121.

Chapter 9

Plaistow Christian Fellowship

Newham, London

Helen Bonnick

Plaistow Christian Fellowship is set in the London borough of Newham, one of England's most deprived boroughs. As Helen Bonnick explains, its work is based on the four aims listed below. Through a multi-talented, diverse membership, these aims are revealed in a wide-ranging and practical ministry to the borough: members worship together, decorate and renovate each other's houses, commit themselves to an understanding and support of Christian work overseas, develop networks with other churches and train Christian leaders.

Plaistow Christian Fellowship is pastored by Terry Diggines, who works closely with a team of several other leaders. Terry and Pat have two teenage daughters. Helen Bonnick, a part-time social worker in Newham, who wrote this chapter on behalf of the fellowship, is married to Steve and has one young son. Like many others in the fellowship she enjoys DIY home improvement.

1. To honour God and to enjoy him.
2. To be committed to the body of Christ worldwide.
3. To be effective in the life of Newham in building the kingdom of God and showing to the community a Christian lifestyle.
4. To have a leadership that reflects the make-up of Newham.

Each monthly edition of *PCF News* begins with this purpose statement of the fellowship. Next follows a list of the leaders' names and telephone numbers: Terry, the pastor (commonly known as Tel), and Pat Diggines, Jacob, Jayne and Peter. Terry and Pat work full time for the fellowship whereas Jacob, Jayne and Peter also have other employment. Thereafter there is no let up—pages crammed with dates to remember, birthdays, testimonies, recipes and puzzles. Letters are printed from folk who have gone abroad. There are reports of church events, reviews, articles on such things as Valentine's Day, vegetarianism and the London marathon, series entitled 'This is my Life' and 'I found It', people recounting their experiences of the truth of Scripture, as well as 'for sale' ads and pictures. Almost everyone has either written or been written about, from the eldest—ninety-year-old Lilian—to the youngest—four-month-old Lucy. Russell (aged four-and-three-quarters) confided in us last year that his hobbies including kissing his sister Bex; other articles in the same issue taught us exactly where Malaysia is and exhorted us to read the labels and consider more carefully what we eat since our bodies are a God-given responsibility.

PCF News reflects the wealth of interests, talents, humour and experiences in the fellowship and goes a long way to foster an understanding of us as individuals and as a fellowship, though it is also important to know about the area in which we live, work, rest, play and worship. In this chapter I want to introduce Plaistow Christian Fellowship to readers who don't receive the *News*!

If you expect an inner-city church to meet in an old, dirty, tumble-down building in an area of close-packed housing, narrow streets and little open space, you would be disappointed by Plaistow Christian Fellowship. Since July 1982 we have been one of a number of different denominations and fellowships meeting in Lawrence Hall, a modern sheltered housing complex and community centre just off the main Barking Road. The road has quite large, generally terraced houses with gardens. Many of the fronts are newly painted; the road is lined with trees, and it is just a five-minute walk to the nearest park where we often meet for worship in the summer.

But the façade can be deceptive. If you stood outside the main entrance and looked down the road you would see a handful of the borough's 100 or more tower blocks. You might perhaps have joined us in watching Ronan Point being demolished because it was literally falling apart. Many homes are old, built in the early part of this century. A large number suffered bomb damage in the war and some still lack a bathroom or inside toilet. Visitors to the area comment on the dirt and rubbish, the noise, the damaged pavements and roads, broken or boarded-up windows, children wandering the streets during school hours, and on how old and ill many people seem.

The London borough of Newham—stretching from the Thames in the south to the original limits of Epping Forest in the north, and home of West Ham Football Club—ranks by the government's own 1986 statistics as England's second most deprived borough. With a population of about 208,000 (at the 1981 census), it has some of London's worst housing problems including hundreds of people without a proper home of their own, high unemployment (as much as 25 per cent in some parts), a higher than average proportion of single-parent families, old and crumbling schools which some children do not attend at all, and growing social stress caused by such multiple deprivation.

Plaistow sits not quite in the centre of the borough, between the predominantly white south with its mass of tower blocks, and the broader streets to the north where a large number of Asian families have made their homes and businesses. Many of the older people were born in the homes in which they still live, though their families may now have moved further out. Into this relatively settled community has also come a variety of younger people: students, hospital workers, those who have chosen to live in the area where they work, shopkeepers and those who have no choice or cannot afford to live elsewhere. There has been a history of mission involvement in the area, the Mayflower Centre and West Ham Central Mission being probably the best-known examples. But since the war church attendance has steadily declined. Even with the recent growth of new or renewed fellowships it has been estimated that not more than 4 per cent of the population attends public Christian worship on a Sunday.[1]

Plaistow Christian Fellowship is one of a number of churches in Newham owing its origins to In Contact Ministries, which seeks to plant new inner-city churches among the ethnic minorities and people of other faiths. From a handful of people meeting together in 1978 in a redundant Anglican church building, the fellowship had grown to about seventy by 1982. People were attracted through formal and informal evangelistic events: coffee mornings, Bible studies, services and missions, as well as by word of mouth. Perhaps the largest proportion of conversions was of friends or family of those already attending, and despite the original aspirations the church remained predominantly white.

By 1982 we had developed a distinctive pattern of worship and leadership and the request of the trustees for an alternative use for the buildings precipitated our move into independence. Leaving a group of In Contact workers to continue their task we came to the brighter, more accessible community buildings, taking our new name as we came. 'We shall go out with joy and be led forth in peace,' we sang as we moved, and that was to be our theme tune for some time, helping us through the problems of birth.

About sixty people made the move. Some of the original members have since moved away, for a number of reasons. Ten people are able to say that they have been involved from the start in one way or another. The others of the 100 (including children) currently on our membership list have either moved into the area, been born or born-again since. Only a handful have transferred membership locally. One hundred has seemed to be our maximum attainable number up till now, though it does not in any way represent our total number of contacts—more of that later!

Just as we came forth in joy, though also with difficulties, so during the last five and half years we have felt what might be described as growing pains. We have gone through periods of struggle, spiritually as well as physically, mentally and emotionally, but we have also been able to laugh and celebrate. We have often proved true the writer of Ecclesiastes as we experienced—

> a time to weep and a time to laugh,
> a time to mourn and a time to dance,
> a time to embrace and a time to refrain
> a time to search and a time to give up,
> a time to keep and a time to throw away.
> (Eccles 3:4–6 NIV)

As we have grown and changed, the overriding consideration has always been to seek that which is good and pleasing to God; our purpose statement has provided a focus for thinking, for planning and for prayer.

To honour God and to enjoy him

Our Sunday morning service struggles into life soon after 10.30. The local laid-back attitude to timekeeping conspires with the requirements of non-Christian families, temperamental transport and last-minute dirty nappies to keep us for as long as possible from honouring God together! For some, too, there is a real battle of the mind and spirit each Sunday morning, and we try to help and encourage these people by collecting them. By 10.50 about sixty have usually gathered, though with a young congregation our numbers are considerably depleted during holidays.

There is no typical Sunday morning, though we follow a pattern of having a shorter family service on the first Sunday of each month, joining with another local fellowship for this every second month. A stranger standing outside in February would have wondered what on earth was going on as the hall rang out with football chants and people puffed and blew as we apparently took part in a keep-fit session. Paula the clown had lost her enthusiasm, but found it at last as she realised how much there was to thank God for. 'Not before time!' some people might have been heard to mutter as they lay slumped in exhaustion!

With a relatively high proportion of illiteracy in the area, considerable effort goes into presenting the message of Jesus in a clear, visual or physical way rather than relying solely on literature. So we use videos, music and movement (as one who takes part I would hesitate to call it dance) to help people understand and remember what is said. The leaders, spouses and those taking part in the service meet early for prayer. We have learned how important it is to claim God's protection on each of us as we join together, and also that each person should arrive already prepared before God. Inevitably this does not always happen; thus the service may be interrupted as we pray with someone who is struggling or respond to another person's worry.

Though we are relatively new as a fellowship and have people from many backgrounds, it would be foolish to pretend that we have no traditions or routines. Indeed, the morning service tends to be quite 'traditional': half an hour of praise, news, prayers, notices and a children's item, usually followed by a sermon lasting about twenty or thirty minutes and a time of open worship. All are encouraged to take part since all are 'ministers', though some do so more than others. It is exciting when new Christians take part, showing a vitality and a refreshing absence of spiritual jargon.

Albert is nearly ninety and only became a Christian in the last five years. He had not been inside a church building for over half his life but was persuaded by a friend to attend a harvest festival service, where he saw something different about the people that attracted him. He has been much sought after in past years as Father Christmas (we almost believe that he is the real one!) and he is valued, too, by us now for the wisdom he brings. When Albert stands up in a service we know that God has something to say to us.

At times the worship seems a real battle and we struggle to understand why this is. Leaving aside the physical distractions of people leaving for a cigarette, babies crying, guitar strings breaking and the fact that some come only as spectators, there is still a sizeable group that desires to meet with God, to enter into his presence, and to bless him. The gifts of the Spirit—tongues, prophecy and healing—are seen, but not always on a Sunday. The disappointment that some may feel perhaps serves as a reminder tht we should seek to worship God each moment of our lives and not only on a Sunday morning. The introduction of a monthly evening praise time has proved more encouraging in this respect, as has our monthly prayer meeting, though whether this difference is because we meet in a smaller group of people, or have a greater expectation or different format, is hard to say.

We try to finish Sunday morning services by 12.15, at which time the children are becoming restless in their groups. But all is not finished and most of us then stay behind to share time, news and food together over a potluck lunch. This varies from week to week: roast chicken and salads or a nutritionist's nightmare of cakes and biscuits.

Mutual encouragement to know God better, for ourselves, takes place in many ways. Most belong to a cell group, meeting weekly. These groups might take up the theme of the Sunday morning sermon in order to develop further the teaching and ideas, but there is room for flexibility so that cell group members can get to know and serve one another better. Even in a fellowship the size of ours it is not possible to know everyone equally well, and cell groups are important for all, but particularly those who are stuck indoors, have few friends or see no one the rest of the week. There are also special teaching sessions from time to time on particular themes: the role of women, identifying and using spiritual gifts, worship; and groups of two or more often meet on their own initiative for discipleship, to study God's word together, or simply to go swimming. Other groups (eg men, young mothers) emerge and disappear as need dictates.

An important aspect of sharing together in the past has been a church weekend away, with a full programme of teaching, games and of course food. Some of the children in the fellowship have never been outside London and so for them it has been a very special experience. One memorable comment came from a four-year-old, breathing his first fresh air as we drove towards Sevenoaks: 'Yuck, it smells funny.'

The church weekend may come but once a year, but services in the park and days out in the summer come round more often. They provide a chance to forget the hole in the roof, the lack of a garden, the traffic fumes, the noisy neighbours, and to relax, throw someone in the boating lake, feed the squirrels and indulge in that most famous of local sports—football. (Whose turn is it to be West Ham this time?) Bruised and battered we queue later at casualty and give thanks in all things!

Jesus demands that his followers surrender their entire lives to him and we have as a fellowship spent time considering the implications for us. We can honour or dishonour God in the way we use our time, our money, possessions and talents as well as our bodies. To acknowledge Jesus as Lord of our homes and finances can be liberating. Though we cannot say that we have everything in common as did the first Christians of Acts, many have, however, opened their homes to others. Those with cars have insured them for any driver or offered a taxi service, and some have cooked meals for other families. Babysitting has been an invaluable service, and we have discovered the value of giving time just to visit and to listen.

We have enjoyed both God and one another as we have worked on each other's homes, decorating or even rebuilding. Some have learned new skills. Many have benefited from Terry's plumbing experience. In an area of poor housing but high prices we have worked wonders on a few homes through working parties, sometimes late into the night. Once, Kim's parents were due to arrive from America the next day and the hall was still unpapered, the living-room unpainted and every room coated in dust. But we finished everything and celebrated with drinks and photos before crawling home!

The spiritualist church down the road has a firm foothold in the area. Terry estimates that 80 per cent of the local people have had some involvement in the occult. Those in the fellowship who have been involved in the past have found daily obedience a struggle at times. We are very aware of the spiritual battles going on around us and the need of God's protection.

On two or three Sundays over the last year we have sought to proclaim God's victory, praising God as we marched and sang as a fellowship around a particular estate. Others have prayed as they walked around on their own. Far from being the great ordeal many expected, it has lifted our spirits as people have come to their windows or gates to watch and wave, and as children have joined us on their bikes. Through these marches and other activities we have got to know the people on the estate and have had the pleasure of seeing them join us on other occasions.

Some have found God's demands on their lives too painful and have chosen the 'easier' way of their former lives, but they are few, and even some of these remain in contact either by friendship or family ties. None of us is perfect, and all of us are aware of the pull of old ways and old friendships. Pat and Terry in particular have missed sleep in order to rescue people physically or spiritually. Prison visiting, psychiatric appointments, drug and alcohol counselling, support for those struggling in their marriages, attending case-conferences for a child in care, providing a character witness, debt counselling—at times these big responsiblities seem a daily demand, and there is a danger that as we focus on the dramatic, others can feel left out, or that we ignore the small, private problems. But we also learn not simply to depend on the formal leadership to teach, correct and counsel. All of us can hear God when we allow him to speak, and each of us can be used by God in serving others.

Great contrast exists within the fellowship in terms of income—from a family of four dependent on dad's dole money to married couples both earning comfortable salaries. (We have no managing directors!) With the distinction further drawn between the more well off young and the less well off older people, a danger of division arises. So much depends on attitudes, expectations or prejudices, but as we get to know one another better we hope that these are overcome. Our giving as a fellowship is testimony to the way God has worked in our pockets. Although we now pay only two full-time workers (Terry and Pat and their family), rather than the original four, we do so (we hope) in a more generous and realistic way. From our weekly offering, averaging about £200, also comes rent and regular support for a number of members and ex-members engaged in Christian ministries as well as the more mundane stationery, printing and refreshment expenses. We just manage to balance the books each year, but there is also much giving and sharing that never appears in the accounts.

Is it the enjoyment of God which sets apart the new and renewed churches from the more conventional? Many of us have experience of churches where enjoyment was the last thing on people's minds. In Plaistow we have learned that there may seem little in our daily lives to enjoy—friends, neighbours and children suffer abuse, harassment and the stress of inner-city life—but God is good: he comforts us; he protects us; he never fails.

To be committed to the body of Christ worldwide

There are currently thirteen people in the fellowship originally from overseas. Six of these have married British folk and will now stay. Some came as students or as teachers in a local missionary training school, and their future is less certain. A few came as children with their own parents from the West Indies. In the past (before the government tightened up the visa regulations) we have had many student nurses, generally from Malaysia or Singapore. Some have become Christians in this country. Others have found the fellowship invaluable in strengthening their faith before returning to homes where they may be ostracised for their beliefs and expected to take part in ancestor worship with the rest of the family. As we have got to know one another better, we have expanded not only our knowledge of geography but also our awareness of, and affiliation to, Christians in other parts of the world.

From our early days as a fellowship we have enjoyed links with Agape International Training (part of Campus Crusade for Christ) who until recently ran a training school in Plaistow for prospective missionaries. Steve and Miriam, with their young daughter Aimee, have led the team for some time, and other teachers and trainers have also stayed with us. Generally we've had two fifteen-week training sessions a year, with any number of students—from four to ten—learning about living in a different culture. Through this we have been enabled to broaden our horizons and have benefited from the additional teachers and the wide range of other gifts brought in. An outside perspective has brought encouragement and also challenged us not to take things for granted. One of the past students, Ute, has regularly updated us on her experiences as a health worker in an isolated mountain region of Uganda and more recently back home in West Germany when the African situation became too dangerous.

Once a month in our Sunday service and three times a year in our prayer meeting we focus on Christians overseas. It is rarely a dry or boring time with so many personal contacts to remember, though the experience is more real for some than for others. Greg helps to bring to life the situation in India, having spent over a year there with VSO, and Melanie has a wealth of stories from her time with YWAM and afterwards with a family in Holland.

But for us 'worldwide' does not just start at Calais. We are conscious of the need to develop links with, and commit ourselves to, Christians outside our own tiny patch. Those moving into Plaistow may still have contact with their churches of origin (often providing great contrast and even conflict in terms of lifestyle and cultural norms) or with friends in other parts of the country. Terry and Pat, too, have been asked to teach at other church holidays, conferences and in a special way as trustees of Anapauo, a Christian retreat centre in Suffolk whose name means 'come aside and rest awhile'. Various members of the fellowship work with London ECUM (the Evangelical Coalition for Urban Mission), Scripture Union, Frontier Youth Trust and Newham Youth for Christ. All these groups also encourage us to lift our eyes above the borough boundaries and provide a more accessible forum for the sharing of ideas, needs and resources.

As an inner-city church we may seem in some people's eyes to be relatively poor, but God has opened our eyes to bring an understanding, too, of our many riches. We need to receive from other fellowships, but we also have much to give. We are all part of the same body worldwide. As Paul reminded the Corinthian church, we suffer with our brothers and sisters wherever they are, but we also share in their happiness.

To be effective in the life of Newham

We believe that there are particular features about Newham which make our aim both crucially important and often painfully difficult. Each day we meet people who feel trapped by their circumstances. Victims of bad housing conditions and an inadequate social security system, suffering from (or themselves perpetrating) violence, arson, and racial attacks—many simply give up hope. Crime, drug and alcohol abuse make life more tolerable for some. Others give up altogether and join us via the local psychiatric hospital. As I've already mentioned, the attraction of the occult is strong, and people have experienced apparent healing and comfort as they have looked for something more powerful than the local government to bring relief.

To be anything other than a select club we therefore need to present a God who is real and who is alive. We should not be simply superimposing our faith on to local, predominantly working-class culture, but presenting an honest and exciting way of living based on Christ's teaching and on our relationship of love and obedience to him. I use the words 'need' and 'should' intentionally—easy to say but much harder to do. Old ways of thinking and doing are hard to shake off. In doing what we believe to be God's will we can find ourselves at the receiving end of much criticism from inside as well as outside the church. We grow weary and are discouraged when we do not see 'results'. Some find the cost of commitment to the tough area of Plaistow too high and move away. In such a situation we have to trust God that we are being effective. Fortunately we are not alone.

We have his Holy Spirit, and we also have one another.

Many churches within Newham have made a clear and determined effort over the last few years to shed the practice of each building its own little kingdom, so that there is now a series of overlapping networks of churches meeting regularly across denominations and across the borough. These are based, of course, on a shared knowledge and love of God, but also on the development of personal relationships among the leaders and increasingly among the congregations. PCF is involved particularly with a group of about ten fellowships which have taken the name of Newham Christian Fellowships.

Beginning from the leaders meeting regularly for prayer, there are now joint prayer meetings, celebrations, evangelistic events, teaching seminars and an annual march of witness, on some occasions linked with a float in the town show. Naturally enough, not all agree on every issue, but together we balance one another and have much to give and to learn. This unity is important since a greater number of people are able to present a message to the borough which is therefore less easily ignored. Together our numbers justify hiring the town hall for teaching, carol services and worship. In February 1986, on a memorable occasion, representatives of over thirty fellowships met across racial and denominational boundaries to repent of our past attitudes of mistrust and prejudice and to affirm our unity in Christ.

Being committed to the life of Newham has meant different things for different people. Staying put can be hard with old friends and haunts around or with the kids' education to consider. Many decide to do so, nevertheless, and others have moved in to live among the people for and with whom they work. As well as being involved with family, friends or neighbours, we support local organisations and activities, and some have sought to affect the decision-making of the council. With so many different interests involved—the unemployed, school governors, those engaged regularly in evangelism, mothers with young babies, and those committed to their careers, to name but a few—it is not possible to point in one direction and say, 'This is our priority.' Together, though, we are united in a desire to bring *shalom*, or wholeness, to the community, working for justice, peace and healing in whatever way we can.

PCF News has carried a series of articles under the general heading 'Salt of the Earth' in which different individuals have written about ways in which they are acting as an antiseptic, a preservative, a flavouring (a colouring?—no artificial additives here!) to those with whom they mix daily. In her post in a large local comprehensive, Jayne has tried to show respect to the pupils and in so doing has gained the trust and friendship of many children. Recognising her Christian faith they often go to her for help in times of trouble, be it academic, emotional or physical, seeking her advice, too, on issues such as sex before marriage and family life. Other members of the fellowship also count such lifestyle evangelism their main priority, while some are committed to a regular programme of door-knocking and literature distribution. Their tireless efforts bring rewards when people come along to the fellowship. Rather more of us have been involved in following up contacts for particular evangelistic events.

Being salt is not only for those in work. All have a valuable part to play in community life whether informally through friendships and visiting people or through involvement in more formal groups. A major project over the last year has been a link with the local tenants' association. Some people have asked when we hope to take over the running of the group and to make it 'Christian', but this is to misunderstand our intentions. We are open about our faith, but our first role is to serve the community by being available for advice, counselling or transport and by providing workers for their summer play scheme and after-school club. It has been especially exciting when children, parents and members of the committee have then come along to one of our services. In an area where *social* church-going is certainly not the norm and many people have been put off by conventional expressions of religion, it is important that we are seen by others as practical people who genuinely care, who can be trusted.

Social concern, social action or social change can be thankless tasks. A group of eight people hoping to be salt through their involvement in the local Labour party meet monthly to encourage one another, especially Steve—a member of the council—throwing around ideas, considering the implications of various decisions or policies and providing emotional and prayer support.

One part of living in God's kingdom which many desire and yet find so difficult to take hold of is a sense of self-acceptance and self-worth. Past experience for some, or ways of thinking for others, seem to place blocks all along the route. Regardless of age, sex, race, education or background, God loves each of us equally, but too often we do not treat each other accordingly. Those involved in the children's work struggle with how to include them in our worship other than in a token way. When is it right to laugh *with* the kids as they sing (perform?) at the front and when are we laughing *at* them? Is it OK to giggle when we sing 'He's got Vicky's goldfish in his hands'?

A growing number of us have children of our own, and there is often a large group of children whose parents do not attend, some of whom it seems are practically kicked out in the morning and expected to roam the streets. At a recent count we had thirty under-twelves; services have to be relevant to them. We need to provide more than just a baby-sitting service; rather somewhere they can observe and be included in a different way of life, a different set of values and worshipping the living God. In the past we have failed to meet the needs of teenagers because of a lack of facilities and a need for special skills and understanding. Soon we shall have to meet this challenge again.

Are we being effective in our involvement in the borough? We can look at our 'successes' and encourage one another that we are, but when we look outwards at the people in need of so much, we can feel ineffective. We long to see God at work (even more than we do already), breaking into people's lives in a real, miraculous and healing way.

To have a leadership that reflects the make-up of Newham

This aim is causing some problems since the fellowship as a whole is slanted towards one section of the community. Nevertheless, it remains a goal that is important for us to keep in mind.

In common with many churches in the borough, PCF has a gap in the middle age range, from about forty-five to sixty-five, a shortage of white working-class men and, as a church with predominantly white leadership, an under-representation of Asian and Afro-Caribbean members. Despite concerted efforts over the years we have also failed to attract many from a group of people who might conveniently be called the 'happy pagans', that is those in satisfactory housing with a relatively stable family life, probably in employment and living their lives without recourse to outside support. It seems that people in this group require something dramatic to happen before they recognise a need for God in their lives. God longs to see them come to him, however, and so do we! These are people with talents and skills not yet to be found in the fellowship, and we are challenged as we think not only of what they may become in Christ, but also of how we may as a fellowship be enriched by their presence. Until we are truly representative, we will continue to experience a real loss in terms of the energy, resources and experience such people can bring. Part of the mosaic is missing.

Our main leadership also still falls short in reflecting the make-up of the fellowship itself. Terry and Pat, the only two ex officio members of the leadership of five, can call themselves 'local' with some justification, Terry having been brought up in the adjoining borough and both having lived in the area for the last seventeen years. But the other three leaders (who stand for a four-year period with the possibility of returning later) are all of a similar age, later twenties/early thirties, and are from outside the East End and in work. In seeking to redress the balance, we have tried hard to train people through other leadership roles and tasks (cell groups being the best example).

We like to think that leaders are 'recognised' rather than simply chosen. Members of the fellowship are asked to suggest people who they believe already exercise a leadership gift, and the leaders' group then makes the final decision, talking and praying with those suggested. Leadership is shared, although Terry is the official pastor. Although different gifts are exercised equally within the leadership and decisions are shared, it is also true that Terry fulfils a slightly different role in view of his greater availability. If he and Pat moved away it would be almost impossible at present to find others to take their place.

We have sometimes been left with a gap for a short while until a new leader has been found, but we are now about to face some more urgent thinking as Jacob reaches the end of his stint, Jayne takes a year out following the birth of her baby, and Terry and Pat have a long-deserved sabbatical. Meetings have been held long into the night to consider the problem. Each time, though, we return to the same conclusions: despite our best intentions we have failed adequately to follow through the training and equipping of people to take on church leadership. Thus we have also been forced to consider other questions: is our idea of the way we think things should be done different to the way God intends? Is he trying to show us people whom we have simply overlooked? We see people who have a real love for God, with a developing maturity, sticking power and obvious pastoral concern. They may have been 'leaders' of families or among their friends, but how would they cope in an arena which has been until now totally alien, and for which they have not been adequately prepared? Other folk appear to be suitable and yet decide themselves that leadership is not for them, perhaps because of anxiety about the time commitment or a lack of confidence in themselves.

We are still struggling with these issues and do not yet have the magic solution; but as we tackle them we know that we must look again at our training programme, at our methods of choosing people for leadership, and at the tasks we expect our leaders to do. As we learn from God we are encouraged rather than discouraged, however, and we continue to hope that one day we will have a leadership which is truly representative of the borough. Vital though the overall leadership is, there are other important tasks to engage in.

We try to get away from the idea of a hierarchy, though perhaps rather unrealistically. Each of the six cell groups has shared leadership which is responsible for weekly organisation and delegation as well as for providing a level of pastoral care for members. We have a church administrator, and others have responsibilities for finance, children's work, music, the magazine or evangelism. The drawing up of rotas is another important task, and sometimes people are asked to do one specific job. Most people are involved in one way or another, though as usually happens a small core of people is involved in most activities. Whether or not we are formally recognised, however, each of us is valuable to God and to one another, and each is vital to the growth and building of the body. Each of us has gifts, and we aim to value all equally as we hear from one another, pray for each other and enjoy being together.

Inner cities are areas of great diversity and change. People of all different backgrounds come and go. Those with strong commitments to the area live alongside people for whom it is simply a staging post. At PCF we hope to reflect this diversity and also to learn from it. We do not want to get stuck in a rut. There can be great potential for conflict in terms of age, race, culture or occupation, but there is also great potential for growth if we seize the opportunity to learn from one another. Sometimes nothing seems straightforward or to be taken for granted, but the challenge for us as Christians is to bring to life Christ's teaching about repentance, about obedience and about unity; to draw our strength from God and to encourage one another; to present to those around us a God who is real and relevant.

As a fellowship we have been both individually and corporately shaped by our social environment, but we seek also to shape it and to experience God's breaking into the lives of people in Plaistow, bringing healing and forgiveness and hope. This then is our priority for the future.

Note

[1] Driscoll and Smith, *West Ham Christians 1984: A Summary of the Report to the Archbishop's Commission on Urban Priority Areas* (London ECUM: 1984).

Chapter 10

St Agnes, Burmantofts, Leeds

Chris Burch

Maggie Durran aptly describes St Agnes, near the centre of Leeds, in her book The Caring Church. *'The parish ... presents the visitor with the contrasts of large, green expanses overshadowed by high-rise flats; new, neatly packed streets of council and private dwellings, old and sometimes dilapidated Victorian terraces and streets of shops ... The church itself is a small, blackened building, its spire now an incongruous landmark...' Incongruous as the building may be, there is nothing incongruous about the Christian love and warmth radiating within and from this church. Worship is the fountain-head and core of the church's life, and out of it grows a sense of peace in Christ that holds together despite the destruction and pressures all around.*

Chris Burch and his wife Roz came to the parish in 1982. 'Whatever else St Agnes may be, it's never dull,' Chris comments. Six weeks after their arrival Martin was born, then Rebecca two years later. As a family they enjoy playing with their new computer, travelling in the country and singing.

The parish

Roughly two miles outside the city of Leeds, Burmantofts parish covers only half a square mile but its four estates are home for 6,500 people. Traditional back-to-back houses march over the northern part of the parish: small they may be, but it's easier to heat a house with only one outside wall! South of these is a large council estate built in the 60s and 70s: part houses and part tower blocks; and towards the city centre is the third estate: Ebor Gardens. Here council flats and maisonettes went up fast in the 60s' building boom; but now, in the 80s, despite obvious neighbourliness, we find decay and many rootless, single people. Meanwhile, the fourth and smallest estate is isolated from the other estates by the huge Burtons complex which occupies a good third of the total parish area. The 'Torres' consists of pre-war council houses where it is harder to keep house and to shop than anywhere else in the parish.

Living in Burmantofts

It's fashionable to portray inner-city areas as places of unrelieved gloom. Not so in Burmantofts. How many parishes have not one but two wet fish shops?—one old-established fishmonger who boasts 'If it swims we sell it!', and another newer shop that has opened in the last five years.

Harehills Lane, on the north-eastern boundary of the parish, must be one of the best shopping areas outside the city centre. Apart from the fishmonger's, there's an old-fashioned shoe repair shop, and one of those special shops where you can buy two ounces of lard, or fresh brewer's yeast, or meat paste that the shopkeeper spoons into a pot for you...as well as two or three greengrocers, several good bakers, and the usual supermarket, hardware shop, clothes and wool shops, and several ethnic take-aways. There are

also ten pubs and eleven working-men's clubs in or just outside the parish—but only one post office, where the queues
on pension day are formidable. The bus services are pretty
good—even from the Torres there's a regular bus down
Lupton Avenue into town.

We do not have a large percentage of Asian or Afro-
Caribbean residents, but the biggest 'minority culture' in
the parish is Irish Catholic. Overt Catholic-Protestant prejudice is almost a thing of the past here, but it does seem
difficult to grow beyond superficial politeness in our rela-
tions with St Patrick's Church on York Road. Once, when
a particular Roman Catholic curate and I really did get on
well, and we were working together on a local campaign to
get a pedestrian crossing, we had a drink together in a local
pub. The other pub-goers were obviously surprised, and
later I received an anonymous phone call accusing me of
'consorting with papists'. Perhaps there is real spiritual significance in the ecumenical movement after all…

Odd 'fax' (trivial or otherwise)

Last summer our local ministry team did a study of the
parish profile as part of our training under a diocesan
scheme. We looked up the 1981 census figures; inevitably
they are out of date, but they give an idea of how Burmantofts compares with the average figures for Leeds as a
whole. The population of the parish is 6,500, in 2,900
households. Of these houses, 63% are council owned (compared with the Leeds average of 37%), and 27% are owner-
occupied (Leeds average 54%). In Leeds as a whole, 48%
do without a car: in Burmantofts it is 71%. Over 25% of our
parishioners are of pensionable age (18% in Leeds),
whereas the figures for children are the other way round:
18% in Burmantofts, Leeds average 22%. This last figure
is, of course, most likely to be inaccurate, as families grow
up here faster than they move on. The other figure that is

certainly incorrect is the percentage unemployed. In 1981, the figure for Burmantofts was 15%, compared with a Leeds average of 10%. Our percentage is certainly a lot higher than that now, although we do not have the highest unemployment in Leeds.

S: Agnes Church—a brief history

St Agnes was consecrated on 20th May 1889, having been an offshoot of St Stephen's, further south towards the city centre. At the time it was on the edge of the city, with the workhouse to the west (now St James' hospital) and a fairly new and fast expanding brickworks to the east.

Unlike many of its neighbouring parishes, St Agnes seems to have been self-consciously low church. This term refers less to doctrinal considerations than to the details of dress and ceremonial which were or were not tolerated. I don't know what gospel the first vicar (one Willard Hartley Stansfield) preached, but I do know that the church has never had candles on its Communion table! Some time before the war, the patronage of the church (ie the right to choose the next vicar) passed from an individual to the Church Trust Fund Trust, managed by the Church Pastoral Aid Society, an evangelical body which has given St Agnes its present-day evangelical stance.

During World War II, St Agnes became the garrison church for the Leeds Civil Defence Messenger Corps, a band of teenagers who took messages on bicycles around Leeds during air raids. Some of them still come to the Remembrance Day service, and their colours still hang over the war memorial.

Bryan Ellis

When Bryan Ellis came to St Agnes as vicar in 1962 his

vicarage was two miles from the church and way outside the parish. Within a few years, much of the old-fashioned, densely packed housing had disappeared, a whole society destroyed. Morale was low in the church and in the area; there had been talk of closing the church and merging the parish with St Cyprian's up the road.

But Bryan was, and is, a 'stayer'. He had a mature theology of Christian presence in a post-Christian urban culture, coupled with a growing experience of charismatic renewal, with its promise of spiritual gifts and depth of loving relationships. (It is possible to read directly what Bryan has to say on this; he edited a journal at the time called *Christians in Industrial Areas* and also contributed an article to the Post Green Community's magazine *Towards Renewal*, which was reprinted in *Renewal: An Emerging Pattern*, edited by Graham Pulkingham. He also contributed a chapter called 'The Urban Scene' in *Evangelicals Today*, edited by John King and published by Lutterworth.)

Slowly and painfully, a new spiritual life began to emerge, focused initially on long and costly personal ministry by Bryan and Barbara Ellis, and expanding to include a growing core of committed Christians at St Agnes. The emphasis was heavily on shared love and concern. It must have been heart-breaking to see young Christians, on the verge of flowering into mature individuals in the church, suddenly rehoused out of the area, or falling victim to a broken marriage or unemployment. It still is. But the growth continued.

The late 70s—ministry, money, church interior

By the end of the 70s, St Agnes was moving into new areas of ministry. A team of elders was set up to support and strengthen the vicar, and area house groups were started in four parts of the parish. By now there was a small number of professional 'incomers' in the church, living in or near the parish. They often made significant contributions; but most would move on after a few years. The core leadership stayed (and still stays) mainly with local people who remain in the area.

The diocesan quota was low then, and giving at St Agnes was exuberant. In 1979–80 the PCC gave away something like one-third of its income, including a voluntary extra quota to help parishes struggling to pay theirs! In 1980 the church started an ambitious scheme to reorder the inside of the building. They removed the choir-stalls (the choir having walked out some years before, over the use of renewal songs) and carpeted the chancel, centre aisle and open space at the back.

All the chancel furniture is now movable—preaching-desk, Communion table, chairs etc—so that dance and drama are possible in worship. We've put on concerts in church, too. The grim old vestry is now a pleasant and well used prayer chapel dedicated to St Luke, where people can go during the services for prayer or healing, or to pray quietly at other times.

In January 1981 Bryan and Barbara left for Wakefield, and after a year's gap, I arrived at the boarded up vicarage, fresh and very green from a curacy in south Leeds. My initial impressions were of a warm and friendly church, with a very high level of commitment to each other but a low profile in the area. There was a flourishing corporate ministry, but cracks were appearing in the elders' group, partly through the pressures resulting from being without a vicar for a year, partly from the expectations put on them (unwittingly) by the rest of the congregation. The worship was friendly and laid back. The PCC, aware of the danger of being introverted, had asked for a new vicar to lead them out in evangelism.

A renewed Christian congregation ready to shine out as the light of Christ in the area? Possibly, but problems of survival have never been far away. The financial honeymoon ended. In a year the quota almost doubled.

It is now many times that amount, and we all still live on a knife-edge of insecurity—vulnerable to many pressures from our families, our workplace, the government or city council, or even to upset in the church. For the same Spirit who increases our joy in the Lord and in each other also increases our sensitivity to each other's pain.

Worship

Suppose you live locally and have a sudden rush of blood to the head one Sunday morning. You get up to go to St Agnes for the first time. You mount the steps and pass the iron gates (locked most of the week), through the massive wooden doors and into the church. There's a carpeted open space at the back, with one or two posters on the wall, and several people chatting in small groups. You are welcomed by a couple of sidespeople who hand you two hymnbooks, a Communion service booklet, a weekly service sheet with the order of service and the week's notices, and perhaps a monthly magazine and an alternative eucharistic prayer. You sit in a pew (by yourself), drop the books and sheets, and wonder where everyone else is.

Half a dozen singers and musicians are getting ready in the brightly lit, open-plan chancel in front of you. Just before 10 o'clock they strike up with a lively folk-style song. You hear one or two less tuneful voices singing along behind you, and look round. The church has mysteriously filled up—from a dozen at 9.55, to maybe forty at 10 o'clock. It will be fifty by 10.15, and when the children come in later on there will be sixty or so adults and about thirty children. What's the service going to be like?

Anglican—but...

The service is recognisably Anglican, but even the modern
Alternative Service Book Rite A is a bit wordy in places—
especially the long thanksgiving prayer—with thirty lively
children in church. Our much shorter 'alternative eucharistic prayer', though totally unauthorised, contains all the
bits you find in the longer prayers.

Music

We rate worship very highly, as an activity that (potentially
at least) can bring people together and to God. We therefore try to include our down-to-earth concerns in worship—
often that means noisy children—but also to lift people's
vision to the glory of God. In both these aims the choice of
music is important. We try to blend traditional and modern, intimate and raucous, challenging and reassuring.
Until recently we've found the *Songs of Fellowship* collec-
tions rather bland and have gone instead for the Celebration Communities' books, especially *Cry Hosanna*, which
has a rich collection of songs relating to family, community
and mission in a difficult environment. But we're beginning
to branch out a bit more, using the overhead projector
where a song isn't in any of our books.

Crosses and candles

If you come on Palm Sunday, you'll be given a palm cross to
stick on your wall as a reminder of what Jesus did for you
the first Holy Week. You'll also be given a branch off a local
conifer and asked to join in a swaying, dancing procession
round the church to the strains of 'We cry Hosanna,

Lord'—the only time when dancing in church is not an optional extra! During Holy Week, the children take part in a project each morning called 'Jerusalem Journey', and on Easter Sunday their work is displayed in church for all to see. Last Easter we introduced a huge paschal candle, with ceremonial to match: not really our style, but a dignified and slightly awe-inspiring start to the biggest celebration of the church's year. And on whatever Sunday you come, the last song of the service is led by the children—dozens of them—standing at the front with percussion instruments, or doing the actions, or marching round the church.

Symbols and words

We function on many different levels, don't we? And in a mainly non-book culture, symbols, movements and atmosphere convey more than mere words. Our preaching is therefore the servant of our worship, not its master. But symbols that aren't understood are no good either. So the Advent wreath or the Easter candle are explained very simply—and that explanation becomes the Advent or Easter message.

What might you, as a newcomer, make of it? Would you be intimidated by the building? Or, as we like to think, would you be drawn to the majesty and the warmth of God once you get inside? You're probably a bit mystified by the service, with all its books and strange language. But if you stick around, more of it will become clear. And some casual newcomers do stick around, because in a strange way, people sense the presence of God on Sunday morning at St Agnes. Not a God they can instantly understand, but a God who is less remote than they thought, and more sympathetic. (On this note, you might enjoy the Grove Booklet 'Worship in the City', written by John Bentham, now curate at St Agnes. He's drawn from our experience, and his ideas have also taken us on a step or two.)

Activities and organisations

The Sunday morning service is the summit of all our activity—the fountain-head of our blessing from God, and the focus of our self-offering to God. And it involves a huge amount of work for many people. Apart from clergy and musicians, there are rotas for sidespeople (your first welcome to the church—very important), creche helpers for the under-fours, and coffee or tea after the service (so you can get to know us a bit). Also, four adults spend a term at a time teaching the four to ten-year-olds, and there are rotas for reading Bible passages and leading intercessions. The rotas often clash—one church member found she was helping in the creche, reading the Gospel and doing coffee all on the same morning! Oh, and I forgot, a smaller number of people share in the distribution of Holy Communion, and others wait in the prayer chapel to pray with and lay hands on those who want healing.

Mid-week gets a bit hectic sometimes too. Those in leadership could find themselves at two or even three meetings in a week, which is a lot when you've been working hard all day. But there aren't so many church members with the confidence, experience and energy to share the really responsible jobs around. (Sounds as if we need to look at our lay training!) The Old Testament talks about a year of jubilee, when the whole land rests and is restored. We have fantasies about a jubilee year St Agnes-style—ie free of all business meetings...

I envy churches that have scrapped all their organisations, but our organisations express and channel our life. It's at the house groups and women's Bible study that people not only read the Bible together, but also share their deep concerns. It's at the young people's clubs, Explorers and Pathfinders, that local kids can see how Christian adults relate to them—to the imperfect glory of God! And it's at the recently launched community project that we've put our faith to the test in the irreligious world of daily work—of time-sheets, supervisors and verbal warnings— where relationships of Christian trust have to cope with the Manpower Services Commission, bureaucracy and sheer human cussedness; where love has to become more than mere sentiment, and we learn to cope with conflict and reconciliation.

Leadership

The PCC is the decision-making body in the church. It can reach heights of vision and unity, and descend to pettiness and self-interest. But a really bad meeting usually leads us to work through the difficulty, not to pretend it isn't there. A recent example of this was the row two years ago about the local ministry team.

The local ministry team is the child of a union between our original elders, set up by Bryan Ellis, and the diocesan local ministry scheme, set up more recently by the Bishop of Ripon. We joined the diocesan scheme, but saw ourselves initially as more or less in continuity with the eldership, except that we were officially recognised, and an outside tutor came to train us. (The clergy learn with the rest of the team.)

Two years ago we asked the PCC for permission to enlarge the team. The meeting was confused and unhappy: it turned out that the team had inherited a tag attached originally to the elders, almost that of a 'secret society'. We sought the help of the diocesan organiser for local ministry to work through the confusion from first principles. A load of stuff emerged, things people felt but hadn't expressed, about the vicar's role, about the way elders should be chosen, about what they should do, and so on. Eventually we were able to move consciously away from an eldership model, chosen by the vicar and geared to strengthening and enlarging his ministry, to a local ministry model, chosen by the church and geared to help the church fulfil its ministry.

Since then the team has had a more settled life. We've not felt it so necessary to justify our existence, since our 'success' is seen in the effective ministry of others, not of ourselves. And that, as you can imagine, is quite liberating. We spend much of our time doing training modules supplied by the diocese. Often we choose these to help us tackle a current live issue. A recent example is baptism and the pastoral care of children. Other sessions are spent checking on the pastoral care of the congregation, or sharing wisdom on difficult pastoral issues, or suggesting people for jobs that need doing. Every meeting starts with an extended time of prayer. Our first tutor put the wind up us about our shallow prayer life, and we've never forgotten the lesson!

Are we as a church trying to do too much? Certainly we feel under constant pressure—our vision and imagination clashing with our lack of numbers and resources, and the continual need to work through our own weaknesses and problems. But we can no longer be called inward looking.

Reaching out

God's commission to us for the area is a double one—to be *servants* in a way that demonstrates what God's kingdom is about, and to be *witnesses*, pointing people to Christ, and inviting a response. It's fair to say we find serving easier than witnessing—but that's not for want of trying.

Evangelism

Much has been written about the difficulty of authentic evangelism in Britain's urban priority areas. The church is often the greatest obstacle: because of its cultural history it has been identified with the establishment, with the articulate, comfortable middle class. But without the church there can be no gospel, for it is Christ's body that makes the Word flesh, even today. We have been involved in three large-scale city-wide evangelistic campaigns in the last five years. We benefited from the experience by discovering unknown and untapped gifts in our own fellowship—but I have to say that the impact on the area was small. Although this isn't a universal experience (one inner-city church in south Leeds has recently 'taken off' in effective evangelism as well as caring and serving), it is common. We as a church need to *become* good news, if our words about the good news are to ring true.

Service

Much of our service in the area springs directly out of our life together. Monday Break, our mothers and toddlers group, has fostered a wholefoods co-operative that buys in bulk, packages and distributes additive-free food at a price we can all afford. One leader in the church has resigned from the local ministry team to pursue a vocation to politics. She sees it as her way, in Christ's name, to encounter both the multitude of individual needs that never come near the church, and also the corporate disease of our society, by being creatively involved in the way decisions are taken. Her choice to leave wasn't easy for some of us to accept (myself included). But the problem was one of emotion, not of principle. (Indeed, there are several political activists at St Agnes—not all in the same party.)

My own ministry includes a fair bit outside the church. Being a vicar gives me opportunities in local schools, for instance, where I am known (admittedly superficially) by all but the Roman Catholic kids. The local probation officers and I have started a community helpers lunch which I chair. It has enabled workers from many different agencies to get

to know each other without having to go through the usual
channels. Then there's our regular, patient work with
people who come for baptisms, weddings and funerals—
perhaps we don't follow up those contacts as we should, but
they are part of a loose network of relationships: people to
people, and people to God.

There are the more traditional organisations—youth and
children's clubs for instance—which serve the young, and a
growing pastoral ministry to serve the old. Two church
members are about to start advice sessions in the Ebor Gardens community centre, helping people sort through problems with money, bureaucracy, etc. Others are involved
with justice and peace issues, locally and internationally,
through Christian organisations we support.

I've already mentioned our community programme. It's
supervised by a member of our local ministry team and
employs ten people to decorate houses and flats for elderly
and disabled people who couldn't do it for themselves.
Only a drop in the ocean? Yes, but a sign of the kingdom of
God too, and a signpost, a pointer for others.

Relations with other churches

Our local Anglican neighbours either admire what we're
doing, or think we're quite mad. Until recently we had the
equal highest giving per family in the deanery—a deanery
that includes some of the wealthiest parts of Leeds. Since
Faith in the City, the suburban churches are showing signs
of wanting to help a bit more. But my clergy colleagues
have some strange suspicions about what we get up to—
whatever does the word 'renewal' conjure up in people's
minds? Or perhaps it's the way I come over at clergy meetings? But the bishops and other church officials are very
supportive—both personally and financially—within the
limits of the system.

We have an informal clergy fellowship that meets

monthly and includes local Roman Catholic and Methodist clergy as well as a couple of Anglicans. We had close links with a local Baptist church, which became unviably small two years ago and decided to close. The Yorkshire Baptist Association has not given up, however; they are holding, not dispersing, the money they raised from selling the building, and are waiting for a suitable opportunity to help support a Christian presence in Ebor Gardens estate again, we hope on an ecumenical basis (ie with us). Meanwhile, they are being most supportive of us (for example, by financial help for the advice sessions).

So is St Agnes good news in the neighbourhood? My conclusion, at the moment, is 'Yes—but not enough people can see it.' Those who are impelled to come to church may well meet the living God through worship or welcome or friendship or healing. But our vision for the future is for the good news to be apparent in the whole area, conveyed through Christ's people, not inside, but outside the church building.

Listen to the Spirit

What is the Holy Spirit saying to the churches? To St Agnes, I guess he is saying, 'In quietness and confidence shall be your strength' (Is 30:15 AV)—though entering the gates of peace often takes a titanic struggle! We need to deepen our roots in God, and so to find his strength and love for our own growth and healing, as well as for our task in the area.

But what is the Spirit saying through us to the rest of the church? Without presuming to do his work for him, I would draw a visitor's attention to the place we give to *children*— as present not future members of the fellowship, to our willingness to work with and learn from *other traditions* and organisations, and to our mix of *spiritual and social* concerns. Above all, I would point out that under Christ one inner-city congregation has *survived* all the urban destruction that's come to it, and that it now lives and serves in his name; that *local people* can grow into leadership—without minimising the vital help given by professional incomers; and that God's work in this inner-city area, when given *plenty of time* and a *capacity to suffer* in Christ's name, is bearing lasting fruit.

The Co-publishers

The Co-publishers

British Church Growth Association

The British Church Growth Association was formed in
September 1981 by a widely representative group of Christians committed to church growth either as researchers,
teachers, practitioners or consultants. Following the
Lausanne Congress on World Evangelisation in 1974,
much interest was aroused in church growth thinking,
which in turn led to the first UK Church Growth Consultation in 1978. Also during the 1970s a number of denominations had taken some church growth thinking and
developed it within their own networks. A number of
theological colleges and Bible colleges also began to teach
church growth theory, particularly in their missiology
departments. The Bible Society had begun to develop
church growth courses that were being received enthusiastically. Developments in the work of the Evangelical
Alliance led to the setting up of a Church Growth Unit and

the publication of a *Church Growth Digest*. This unit drew together a number of leaders involved in the church growth field, but it was agreed to widen its impact by the formation of an association which would be even more comprehensive and effective.

Definition

Church Growth investigates the nature, function, structure, health and multiplication of Christian churches as they relate to the effective implementation of Christ's commission to 'Go, then, to all peoples everywhere and make them my disciples' (Mt 28:19). Church Growth seeks to combine the revealed truths of the Bible with related insights from the contemporary social and behavioural sciences. Although not linked to any one school of church growth it owes much to the formulational thinking of Dr Donald McGavran.

Aims

The BCGA aims to help and encourage the church in Britain to move into growth in every dimension. The facilities and resources of the BCGA are available to researchers, consultants, teachers, practitioners and those just setting out in church growth thinking. The Association endeavours to offer practical help as well as encouraging and initiating church growth thinking and research.

Activities

The following are among its activities:
— Producing a quarterly journal particularly geared to the British scene with practical, biblical and theoretical articles

of help to the churches as well as offering a forum for the
sharing of views.

— Producing a number of occasional in-depth papers on a
variety of topics.

— Co-publishing books on church growth.

— Running a specialist church growth book service offering
discounted books to members and producing a catalogue of
recommended church growth reading.

— Operating a reference system for information and per-
sonnel.

— Organising biennial residential conferences on particular topics of church growth relevant to the church in this
country eg Church planting 1983, Conversion 1985, Bridge
Building 1987.

— Encouraging, co-ordinating or organising lectures and
seminars on particular subjects or with particular speakers
which could be of help to the churches.

— Carrying out research in allied fields and building up a
research register of work already done or being undertaken
in various centres.

— Monitoring church growth at home and overseas.

— Linking in with a European initiative to share insights
peculiar to the continent of Europe.

— Encouraging grass-roots involvement through seventeen regional groups.

Government

The Council of the BCGA is made up of fifteen elected
members and seven co-opted members who meet three
times a year. Although members serve in a personal capacity, the Council aims to be representative of geographical
region, denomination and churchmanship, practitioner,
researcher and teacher.

The day-to-day running of the Association is carried out
by an officer with some secretarial assistance and the active

support of members of the Council. The BCGA is a registered charity, no. 28557.

Membership

Membership of the BCGA is open to both individuals and organisations interested in or involved in the theory or practice of church growth. On payment of an annual subscription members are entitled to receive the *Church Growth Digest* (the journal of the Association) four times a year, information about activities through the newsletters, special discounts on conferences and books, membership of the Church Growth Book Service, voting rights to elect members to the Council every two years, links with other researchers, teachers, practitioners, and consultants on a regional or national level as well as help or advice on allied matters.

The current subscription is £8 for individual membership and £17 for organisations or churches.

Further information about the Association and membership is available from the Secretary, British Church Growth Association, St Mark's Chambers, Kennington Park Road, London SE11 4PW. (01-793 0264)

Evangelical Coalition for Urban Mission

ECUM (the Evangelical Coalition for Urban Mission) is a partnership of agencies of similar background and outlook working in varying aspects of urban mission. The member groups retain their separate identities while the Coalition seeks to express and service wider aspects of urban ministry. The Coalition is concerned with the application of the Christian gospel to urban issues which, since the formation of ECUM in 1980, have become of central social, economic and political importance. Below are listed all the agencies in the partnership. Contact National Development Officer, Greg Smith, Scripture Union House, 130 City Road, London EC1V 2NJ (01-250 1966).

ECUM

Evangelical Coalition for Urban Mission
'Christians in Partnership for the Cities' — After reading this challenging book, you will want to respond to the many practical suggestions.
You may want some help from us!
We have—between us—skill, materials and people to help your ministry.

London ECUM

— events
— urban mission resources
— free quarterly mailing
Write to Geoff Thorington, Lawrence Hall, 2/4 Cumberland Road, London E13 8NH (01-476 3651)

Evangelical Christians for Racial Justice

— racial justice based on a clear biblical basis
— monitoring local and national media
— education and training events
— worship and action
— study-pack—*New Humanity*
— magazine—*Racial Justice*
Write to Raj Patel, ECRJ, 12 Bell Barn Shopping Centre, Cregor Street, Birmingham B15 2DZ (021-622 6807)

Frontier Youth Trust

'A missionary association for Christian youth workers'
— eight regional field officers
— training and research
— resources and materials
— events
— FYT News/Information/Updates
— a clearing house for exchanging ideas and experience in youth work
Don't be alone and unsupported in your youth ministry.
Write to Michael Eastman, Scripture Union House, 130 City Road, London EC1V 2NJ (O1-250 1966)

Evangelical Urban Training Project

'Learning without books!'
— urban workshops
— skill training to meet your 'training need'
— training days
— eleven 'DIY' courses
Write to Jim Hart, EUTP, PO Box 83, Liverpool L69 8AN (051-709 1463)

Shaftesbury Project

— biblical and social education and research
— inner-city study group
— papers and study guides
— magazine—*Impact* (with newsletter—*Shaftesbury Project News*, LICC)
Write to Revd Eddie Neale, Shaftesbury Project, Old Rectory, Maid Marian Way, Nottingham NG1 6AE (0602 585731)

City Cries

— Including *ECUM Bulletin*
Stimulate your mind! Share ministries!
— three issues a year on all aspect of urban mission
— book notes
— briefing notes
Write to *City Cries*, Lawrence Hall, 2/4 Cumberland Road, London E13 8NH (01-476 3651)

MARC

Ten Rural Churches

Edited by John Richardson

'Son of man, can these bones live?'

Looking out over the valleys of rural England, Ezekiel might well see the same heaps of dry bones as he described in his prophetic record millenia ago. Yet he might also see those dry bones restored to spiritual and physical life.

Ten Rural Churches invites you to read the stories of ministers from ten British 'valleys' where the drought has given way to young growth. They record the miracles of changing lives against a background that is at once idyllic and brutal. Here lives (and hearts) change slowly, but the Holy Spirit breathes over the cycles of sowing, growing, and harvesting. Does the statistical evidence of decline lead you to despair for the Gospel in rural Britain?

Read this book—and be encouraged.

John Richardson, who has collected these accounts, is vicar of Christ Church, Nailsea, near Bristol. Himself a child of a country market town, he now serves as vice chairman of the Church Pastoral Aid Society evangelism committee and is Resident Chaplain to the Royal Bath and West Agricultural Show. He is also advisor in evangelism in the rural diocese of Bath and Wells and is a founding member of the Federation for Rural Evangelism.

Published jointly with the British Church Growth Association, the Federation for Rural Evangelism, and Church Pastoral Aid Society.